Dear Brothers and Sisters in Christ,

Two thousand years ago, St. Paul who was appointed by God to be the 'Apostle to the Gentiles' was born in Tarsus, in present day Turkey. To mark the bimillenium of his birth Pope Benedict XVI called for a Holy Year from June 2008 – June 2009.

From the moment of his conversion, Paul fearlessly proclaimed the Good News. He sought to take this News into the Gentile world and to build up the Body of Christ beyond the confines of the Jewish community from which he came. For this he journeyed, he suffered, he was martyred. One suspects that were you and I to meet him today, we would encounter an unshakable, almost infectious faith. His was a faith which was permeated with hope: which trusted in the faithfulness of God. He looked to the transforming power of the Holy Spirit, and knew the abiding presence of the Risen Lord who opened the way to the Father and eternal life.

Today, faced with the challenges that agitate the Catholic conscience in our society, the opportunity to reflect on the life and ministry of St. Paul seems especially appropriate. If we are to build up the Body of Christ, if others are to encounter He who is 'wisdom, virtue, holiness and freedom' (1 Corinthians 1:30), our faith and witness must be as convincing as St. Paul's.

My dear people, I ask you to pray for me and for my fellow bishops that we can lead well as you grow in faith and confidence in the Risen Lord. Pray for your priests that they lead you to deeper understanding of God the Father's gift, Jesus Christ. Pray too for yourselves, that you may truly hear Christ's voice and act upon it, using your gifts to help build his Church and to serve the world in which we live (1 Corinthians 12:7).

May God the Father and the Lord Jesus Christ grant peace, love and faith to all of you. May grace and eternal life be with all who love our Lord Jesus Christ (Ephesians 6:23-24).

With my blessing and prayers,

+ Cormac Murphy-O'Connor

Cardinal Cormac Murphy-O'Connor
Archbishop of Westminster

Appointed by God is an opportunity to reflect on our vocation as baptise․
Christians in the light of the writings of St. Paul, apostle, martyr and
evangelist. Running over six weeks, *Appointed by God* includes six session․
for small groups or communities, as well as a series of daily meditations
which you may wish to use on your own.

Weekly Themes

Each week of *Appointed by God* looks at a different aspect of St. Paul's lif․
and writings. Week One looks at Paul the Person; Week Two considers
Paul and suffering; Week Three explores St. Paul and the ideas of myster․
and faith in Christ Jesus; Week Four explores community; Week Five
looks at Paul and righteousness, while Week Six encourages an
exploration of evangelisation through the lens of St. Paul's missionary
endeavours.

Group Reflections

These begin with an opening prayer drawing on the psalms and a few
moments of silence. The opening prayer is followed by a Scripture
passage and a reflection. Following each of these there is an opportunity
for the group to share their thoughts and to explore the implications for
Christian living using the questions provided. The session is concluded
with a series of petitions and a closing prayer.

Daily Meditations

The daily meditations for Sundays provide a background to that Sunday’
second reading. Mondays, Tuesdays, Thursdays and Fridays draw on the
riches to be found in the writings attributed to St. Paul, while Wednesday
will contain a testimony related to the weekly theme. To help our
preparation for the Sunday Mass the Saturday meditation will introduce
the Gospel passage for the next day.

Church documents & Texts

A number of Church documents are referred to in the course of this booklet. You may wish to explore the following further: *Lumen Gentium*, the Second Vatican Council's Dogmatic Constitution on the Church (November 1964); *Apostolicam Actuositatem*, the Second Vatican Council's Decree on the Apostolate of the Laity (November 1965); Pope John XXIII's encyclical *Princeps Pastorum* – on the Missions, Native Clergy and Lay Participation (November 1959); Pope John Paul II's documents *Salvifici Doloris* – on the Meaning of Human Suffering (February 1984), and *Christifideles Laici* – an exhortation on the vocation and mission of the laity (December 1988); Pope Benedict XVI's encyclical on hope, *Spe Salvi* (November 2007) *and the Catechism of the Catholic Church.*

When you pray to God in Psalms and hymns, think over in your hearts the words that come from your lips.

From the Rule of St. Augustine (c. 400)

GW00601190

Initially St. Paul had no desire to be involved in the early Christian movement. On the contrary, St. Paul persecuted those Jews who believed that Jesus was God's promised Messiah (Galatians 1:13; 1 Corinthians 15:9; Acts 22:4). Paul's change of heart came about as a result of divine intervention, a vision of the Risen Jesus and a commission to preach to the Gentiles (Galatians 1:16; Acts 9:1-19; 22:1-16; 26:1-13). Paul's life can be divided into 5 periods.

Period 1	Early Life
c. AD 8	born in Tarsus in Cilicia [modern-day Turkey] (Acts 22:3).
c. AD 20	educated as a strict Pharisee in Jerusalem (Philippians 3:5).
AD 30 – 34	persecuted the new Jewish Messianic movement (Acts 8:3).
AD 34	underwent a conversion experience, was baptised in Damascus, called into Christian ministry and given a commission (Galatians 1:15-16).

Period 2	Preparation for ministry
AD 34 – 37	preached in Arabia and Damascus (Galatians 1:17), returned to Jerusalem.
AD 37 – 48	preached in Syria and Cilicia (Galatians 1:21), settled in Antioch, returned to Jerusalem for the apostolic conference, a meeting with the apostles who had seen Jesus during his earthly life (Galatians 2:1-10).

Period 3   **Itinerant Evangelistic ministry**

AD 48 – 49   preached in Cyprus and southern Galatia = 1st journey *(see map on inside back cover)*.

AD 49 – 52   from Antioch revisited the Galatian churches, preached in Asia, then in Macedonia and Achaia [modern-day Greece] (1 Thessalonians 2:2; 3:1-5), settled in Corinth for 18 months, brought before the proconsul Gallio, returned to Jerusalem (Acts 18:22) = 2nd journey *(see map on inside back cover)*.

AD 53 – 56   revisited the churches, settled in Ephesus for 2 years and 3 months, returned to Macedonia and Asia.

Period 4   **To Jerusalem and then to Rome**

AD 57   returned to Jerusalem with the collection (2 Corinthians 8-9; Romans 15:26; Acts 21:6) = 3rd journey *(see map on inside back cover)*.

AD 57 – 59   arrested in Jerusalem, appealed to Caesar, journeyed to Rome as a prisoner, shipwrecked on Malta.

Period 5   **To Rome, Spain? Rome, martyrdom**

AD 60 – 62   Paul seemed to be under house arrest in Rome (Acts 28:16). It is uncertain if he preached in Spain as was his intention (Romans 15:24).

AD 64   Christians blamed by the Emperor Nero for starting the great fire and many were persecuted (recorded by the Roman historian, Tacitus, Annals, 15:44.2-3). St. Peter was martyred.

c. AD 67   St. Paul martyred (1 Clement 5:5-7) by beheading (Eusebius, The History of the Church, 2:25.5) as he was a Roman citizen (Acts 22:25-29) as opposed to Peter who was crucified.

Opening Prayer

Leader:	I was silent and still; I held my peace to no avail; my distress grew worse, my heart became hot within me.
Group:	While I mused, the fire burned; then I spoke with my tongue: 'Lord, let me know my end, and what is the measure of my days; let me know how fleeting my life is.
Leader:	'And now, O Lord, what do I wait for? My hope is in you. Deliver me from all my transgressions. Do not make me the scorn of the fool.
Group:	'Hear my prayer, O Lord, and give ear to my cry; do not hold your peace at my tears.

From Psalm 39

All:	Glory be to him whose power, working in us, can do infinitely more than we can ask or imagine; glory to him from generation to generation in the Church and in Christ Jesus for ever and ever. Amen.

Ephesians 3:20-21

Let us listen carefully to the Word of the Lord,
and attend to it with the ear of our hearts.
Let us welcome it, and faithfully put it into practice.

St. Benedict of Nursia (c.480-c.547) adapted

Explore the Scriptures Romans 15:14-21

It is not because I have any doubts about you, my brothers; on the contrary I am quite certain that you are full of good intentions, perfectly well instructed and able to advise each other. The reason why I have written to you, and put some things rather strongly, is to refresh your memories, since God has given me this special position. He has appointed me as a priest of Jesus Christ, and I am to carry out my priestly duty by bringing the Good News from God to the pagans, and so to make them acceptable as an offering, made holy by the Holy Spirit.

I think I have some reason to be proud of what I, in union with Christ Jesus, have been able to do for God. What I am presuming to speak of, of course, is only what Christ himself has done to win the allegiance of the pagans, using what I have said and done by the power of signs and wonders, by the power of the Holy Spirit. Thus, all the way along, from Jerusalem to Illyricum, I have preached Christ's Good News to the utmost of my capacity. I have always, however, made it an unbroken rule never to preach where Christ's name has already been heard. The reason for that was that I had no wish to build on other men's foundations; on the contrary, my chief concern has been to fulfil the text: Those who have never been told about him will see him, and those who have never heard about him will understand.

Following a short period of silence you may wish to share an image, a thought, a phrase that has struck you.

Reflection

St. Paul leaves us with great riches both in terms of the letters he wrote and his influence on the members of the Early Church. This influence is strongly felt even today, 2000 years after his birth. In his letters, Paul tells us that he was 'not a polished speechmaker' (2 Corinthians 11:6). If so, he shared with Moses and Jeremiah a lack of oratory skill. Moreover, his opponents testified 'his bodily presence is weak, and his speech of no account' (2 Corinthians 10:10). His confidence and his success came not from himself but from 'the grace of God' that was within him, a 'grace that has not been fruitless' as he risked ridicule and eventually death (1 Corinthians 15:10, cf. Ephesians 3:7). From this we can draw a particularly important lesson for every Christian. The Church's action is effective only to the extent to which those who belong to her are open to the transforming and inspiring power of God's freely given grace.

What is so special about St. Paul, who has been seen as chauvinistic (cf. 1 Corinthians 14) and who from the very beginning has been considered difficult to understand (2 Peter 3:15-16)? Why should we take the trouble to get to know this 'difficult' saint?

The reasons are many. Because, St. Paul was more like us than any of the other apostles in that he had not seen Christ in the flesh. Because, Paul wrote his letters before the gospels were written, providing us with the earliest insight into the Early Church. Because, Paul was first and foremost a pastor and a missionary, a man with very real, practical concerns for the people of God. Paul was an Israelite (Romans 11:1), a descendent of Abraham (2 Corinthians 11:22) who spoke with conviction and from the heart, firmly believing in the power of God to save. Finally, because the 'new life of the Spirit' (Romans 7:6) preached by St. Paul, this new 'life with Christ' (Galatians 2:20), is a constant struggle. Yet, if we open ourselves to God's grace we can be well placed to follow the example of this great 'servant of Jesus Christ' (Romans 1:1). We 'are new born, and, like babies, [we] should be hungry for nothing but milk – the spiritual honesty which will help [us] grow up to salvation' (1 Peter 2:2).

At the important stages of life, at moments of transition and change, do you look to Scripture for inspiration? In times of trouble do you look to Scripture or elsewhere for guidance? What actions and path do you hear God calling you towards?

Leader: Aloud or in the silence of our hearts let us bring to the Father our thanks (pause)…

Leader: In sorrow let us ask the Father for forgiveness (pause)…

Leader: With confidence let us entrust to the Father our cares and concerns (pause)…

Closing Prayer

Heavenly Father,
open our minds and hearts to the working of your Holy Spirit.
Enlightened by Truth and emboldened through Grace,
may faith overcome doubt, love conquer hatred,
hope shine through suffering,
and zeal mark our proclamation of the Good News
that St. Paul preached to the peoples of all nations.
We ask this through your Son Jesus Christ
who lives and reigns with you, in the unity of the Holy Spirit,
one God for ever and ever.
Amen.

Today or over the coming week take a few moments to consider St. Paul's second letter to Timothy (2 Timothy 3:14-17, where he talks about the preparation necessary for leading others to a knowledge of Christ Jesus. Ephesians 6:10-20), too, is a wonderfully rich passage regarding the proclamation of the Good News.

Read the Scripture from 29th Sunday in Ordinary Time (Year A) – 1 Thessalonians 1:1-5

From Paul, Silvanus and Timothy, to the Church in Thessalonica which is in God the Father and the Lord Jesus Christ; wishing you grace and peace from God the Father and the Lord Jesus Christ. We always mention you in our prayers and thank God for you all, and constantly remember before God our Father how you have shown your faith in action, worked for love and persevered through hope, in our Lord Jesus Christ. We know, sisters and brothers, that God loves you and that you have been chosen, because when we brought the Good News to you, it came to you not only as words, but as power and as the Holy Spirit and as utter conviction.

Background

Co-authored by Paul, Silvanus and Timothy, the Church's original evangelists, this letter to the church in Thessalonica, probably written from Corinth around AD 50, is the oldest piece of Christian literature. It is composed in the letter form which was common in the ancient world. It contains an opening greeting (1:1), with a thanksgiving (1:2-5:22) in the main body of the text, and a closing farewell containing a request for prayer (5:23-28). Its purpose is to deal with the theological and pastoral issues confronting the church. Specifically, this letter is concerned with the parousia or the return of Christ (4:13-5:11) and how the community should regard itself as living the Christian life both amongst themselves (4:9-12) and in society (4:1-8).

What separates this letter from 'secular letters' is the claim that the assembly derives its being from God who is declared as 'Father', an ancient Hebrew title (e.g., 2 Samuel 7:14). What differentiates the Thessalonian community from Judaism, however, is the confession and worship of Jesus, who is acknowledged as the Messiah (Christ) who shares in the Lordship of God (see, 1 Corinthians 12:3; Philippians 2:11).

From this greeting all other Christian activity radiates, both prayer and the inner life (1:3) and the public activity of the practice of the faith (1:3). As a result of the foundation of the Thessalonian church a deep communion is established between the activity of the community and the work of the apostolic missionaries. Their Gospel ministry is not merely about human proclamation (see, 1 Corinthians 2:1-2) but concerns the divine work of the Holy Spirit in the midst of the community (1:5a).

Dear Lord and Father,
help us each day to be like perfect children,
help us to shine in the world like bright stars.
Through our words and our actions,
we ask you to bring others to see
your offer of the word of life.
Amen.

Based on Philippians 2:15-16

perfectly well instructed (Romans 15:14)

Having the money, time and the opportunity to study and reflect, St. Paul was well-versed in the Old Testament and the exact observance of the Jewish Law. He was taught by Gamaliel, a member of the Sanhedrin who was a 'Pharisee... a doctor of the Law and well respected by the whole people' (cf. Acts 6:34 and 22:3). Paul was 'perfectly well instructed'. Many of us, however, have not had the same opportunities as Paul. How are we to hand on our faith if we are unable to express what is in our hearts?

In 1980 the Bishops of England and Wales produced a document called *The Easter People* which talked, in part, of everyone's need for continued formation and education in faith. 'Our educational heritage is indeed rich' the document said, reminding us that at the centre of our learning and faith 'is Jesus Christ, teacher and supreme catechist. It is he who will speak to adult and child alike on their pilgrim journey' (*The Easter People*, 155). Education in faith is a life-long process – not ending at confirmation – which needs to remain faithful to the gospel message and be sensitive to contemporary needs and aspirations; it is also a community process where everyone is to be involved.

From the Catechism

133. The Church 'forcefully and specifically exhorts all the Christian faithful... to learn "the surpassing knowledge of Jesus Christ", by frequent reading of the divine Scriptures (Philippians 3:8). "Ignorance of the Scriptures is ignorance of Christ" (St. Jerome)'.

In order to enter more deeply into the life of prayer and to come to grips with St. Paul's challenge to pray unceasingly (1 Thessalonians 5:1), the Orthodox Tradition offers the Jesus Prayer, which is sometimes called the prayer of the heart. Say it often, both out loud and in your heart.

Lord Jesus Christ, Son of God, have mercy on me, a sinner.

The Jesus Prayer, see Luke 17:13; 18:14; 18:3

appointed me as a priest of Jesus Christ (Romans 15:16)

Here Paul talks of his appointment to serve Jesus Christ. His is a special position, an evangelistic and priestly ministry (Romans 15:15-16). However, Paul was very conscious of the difference between himself and the Twelve and of the 'pride of place' they were to be given. Often we can feel that ministry is the special preserve of the 'holy' but St. Paul recognised that throughout his ministry he won, for Christ, the allegiance of the Gentiles by the power of signs and wonders, by the power of the Holy Spirit.

We, like Paul, are given the mandate to witness to Christ, to offer our lives to God. Though we may feel unworthy (cf. 1 Corinthians 15:9), we are called to accept Christ's message and understand that it is a 'living power among those who believe it' (1 Thessalonians 2:13). From the faithful, God calls each of us to a definite service to the Church (Ephesians 4:11-13). We all share in the common priesthood bestowed at baptism and irrespective of vocation, profession, ethnicity or sex; we are called to serve the needy, to spread God's word, to do whatever we do for the glory of God... taking Paul as our model as he takes Christ (1 Corinthians 10:31 and 11:1).

From Apostolicam Actuositatem (On the apostolate of the laity)

3. From the fact of their union with Christ the head flows lay people's right and duty to be apostles. Inserted as they are in the Mystical Body of Christ by baptism and strengthened by the power of the Holy Spirit in confirmation, it is by the Lord himself that they are assigned to the apostolate. If they are consecrated a kingly priesthood and holy nation (cf. 1 Peter 2:4-10), it is in order that they may in all their actions offer spiritual sacrifices and bear witness to Christ all the world over.

Holy Spirit, divine Consoler, O Giver of all supernatural gifts,
I adore You as my true God, with God the Father and God the Son. Grant me
the gift of piety, so that I may serve You.
Grant me the gift of knowledge, so that I may know the things of God.
Grant me the gift of fortitude, so that I may overcome that which threatens
my salvation.
Grant me the gift of counsel, so that I may choose what is from God.
Grant me the gift of understanding, so that I may apprehend the divine and
not the worldly.
Grant me the gift of wisdom, so that I may rightly direct all my actions to God
so that, having loved Him and served Him in this life,
I may have the happiness of possessing Him eternally in the next.
Amen.

St. Alphonsus Liguori (1696-1787) adapted

I've always been a churchgoer without even the usual teenage blip of rebelling. However, it was more a sign of my dutiful spirit than any real living faith. Just as I ate my greens, did my homework and all the other things that I didn't particularly like doing, I went to church. But, my Christian faith was not at the heart of my life. My focus was on having a meaningful job, travelling, meeting interesting people and generally having fun and adventure. I fitted God in round the edges. But because I did go to church and generally led a moral life, I felt I was doing all that was expected of me. It didn't occur to me that there was anything more – that I had actually missed the whole point: that the Christian life is not about spiritual practices and duties but about a love relationship with Jesus Christ who, if you give him permission, floods your whole existence and gives you a totally new perspective on life.

God led me to a place where I had to face myself and my need of him to make sense and meaning of my life. At a charismatic prayer group, I heard Catholics talk about God in a way I had never heard before. I had thought a personal relationship with Jesus was reserved for Mother Teresa types, not ordinary mortals, but the faith of those present made me question my own. I realised I could justify and defend myself or I could admit the truth – that I was empty and hollow inside. For all my outward practices I didn't know God at all. I was faced with a choice. Did I want to run my own life as I had been doing, or was I prepared to hand it over to God and allow his Holy Spirit to direct me instead? Ultimately, this is what being Christian means – trying to live a life, guided by God's Holy Spirit, instead of by human desires, fears and needs. As it says in the Penny Catechism, 'God made us to know him, love him and serve him in this world and to be happy with him forever in the next.'

Kristina Cooper (each of the Wednesday testimonies are taken from www.caseresources.org)

O God, teach me to breath deeply in faith. Amen.

Søren Kierkegaard (1813-1845)

utmost of my capacity (Romans 15:19)

What can we accomplish? What are our limits? Do we need degrees in theology to pass on our faith? Do we think so little of ourselves and our 'capacity' that we fail to act or speak out in groups, or as parents leave the faith education of our children to others?

St. Paul leaves us in no doubt where his great giftedness lies. When he came before the Corinthians he came 'in great fear and trembling' relying not on his own power but on the 'power of the Spirit… the power of God' (1 Corinthians 2:3-5). This same Spirit has been promised to us (John 7:37-39; John 14:16 and Galatians 3:14). Through baptism and strengthened in confirmation, the gifts of the Holy Spirit have been bestowed on us (1 Corinthians 12:4-11). We pray, therefore, that we make the right choices, 'choose the right course' (2 Timothy 4:5) and to use these gifts for the service of others and the Church. When you are next able, read 1 Corinthians 14 and consider how well you are using the talents and gifts you have been given. You may wish to take the time to read and reflect on 2 Corinthians 4:7-15.

Lord, we celebrate the conversion of Saint Paul,
your chosen vessel for carrying your name to the whole world.
Help us to make our way towards you by following his footsteps,
and by witnessing to your truth before the men and women of our day.
Through Christ our Lord.
Amen.

Concluding Prayer, Conversion of St. Paul the Apostle (25 January), Divine Office

Christ's name has already been heard (Romans 15:20)

What would it be like to live in a country where the name of Christ had not yet been heard? More curious still what would it be like to live in a country where Christ's name and words had been heard but are reviled, considered dangerous and thrust underground. Present-day China and Saudi Arabia (in the past the Soviet Union) attempt to repress Christ's message and persecute his followers. However, as the Holy Father reminds us, 'the one who has hope lives differently; the one who hopes has been granted the gift of a new life' (*Spe Salvi*, 2). After the collapse of communism, almost without exception, the countries of the former Soviet Union experienced a 'spring-like awakening' (Russian Orthodox Patriarch Alexei II). The power of the Word of God, survived a time when there seemed to be 'no hope, no God in the world' (Ephesians 2:12).

The spreading of Christ's message to those who have not heard, and those who have heard and yet forgotten, will never be over. Those of us asleep in our faith must awake; relying on others to do God's work is not enough. We are on a real and daily journey towards God. Is there any good reason to ignore the challenge to grow in the light of the gospel?

Now, if you have time and a Bible to hand, read Ephesians 5:14 or read it when you get home.

The kingdom is not only beyond our efforts,
it is even beyond our vision.
This is what we are about.
We plant the seeds that one day will grow.
We water seeds already planted,
knowing that they hold future promise.
We are workers, not master builders; ministers, not messiahs.
We are prophets of a future not our own.
Amen.

Attributed to Oscar Romero (1917-1980)

When the Pharisees heard that Jesus had silenced the Sadducees they got together and, to disconcert him, one of them put a question, 'Master, which is the greatest commandment of the Law?' Jesus said, 'You must love the Lord your God with all your heart, with all your soul, and with all your mind. This is the greatest and the first commandment. The second resembles it: You must love your neighbour as yourself. On these two commandments hang the whole Law, and the Prophets also.'

Matthew 22:34-40

St. Paul, when commenting on Jesus' call to love our neighbour as ourselves, wrote 'Love does no wrong to a neighbour; therefore, love is the fulfilling of the law.' (Romans 13:10). Is our love of neighbour evident in our words and actions? Does the love we have for God shine forth?

O Teacher, Jesus, be favourable to your children.
Grant that we who follow your command
may attain the likeness of your image and
in accord with our strength find in you
both a good God and a judge who is not severe.
Amen.

Clement of Alexandria (c.150-c.211)

In addition to St. Paul's own letters we learn about his life in the writings of St. Luke. The purpose of Luke's writings (St. Luke's Gospel and the Acts of the Apostles) is to demonstrate to Theophilus, Luke's literary patron (Luke 1:3), the basis on which Christianity developed and to highlight the principal features of the Christian movement.

Luke's writings cover the period from the annunciation of the birth of John the Baptist (Luke 1:5ff) to the arrival of St. Paul as a prisoner in Rome (Acts 28:16). Paul enters Luke's narrative at Acts 7:58 where, as a zealous Jew, he consents to the martyrdom of Stephen. From this point until his missionary activity in Cyprus, Luke uses Paul's Jewish name Saul to remind the readers of his Jewish heritage. Luke uses the Roman name Paul when his Christian missionary activity begins (Acts 13:9). Paul's ministry, for Luke, forms part of his overall scheme, the description of God's activity in bringing the Jesus movement to birth in the power of the Spirit (cf. Luke 1:35 with Acts 2:4). For Paul, this ministry begins with his conversion which arises as a result of the direct intervention of the glorified Lord Jesus (Acts 9:4-5). At his direction Saul is commissioned for ministry and baptised by Ananias (Acts 9:15-16, 18).

In Acts 15:36 Luke presents Paul as the principal evangelist to the Greco-Roman world. Occasionally Luke becomes part of the narrative, accompanying Paul on his journeys (Acts 16:10-17; 20:5-8; 13-15; 21:1-8; 27:1-28:16), often fading into the background, especially when Paul gives important addresses (e.g. Acts 20:17-35).

There are two particular difficulties in asking what Luke says about Paul. Firstly, Luke does not reveal that Paul wrote letters to churches and secondly, what Luke tells us about Paul's chronology does not marry precisely with what Paul says himself. In these areas it must be recognised among other things that Luke is interpreting Paul in c.AD80, some 12 or so years after Paul's martyrdom.

Opening Prayer

Leader:	Some wandered in desert wastes, finding no way to an inhabited town; hungry and thirsty, their soul fainted within them.
Group:	Then they cried to the Lord in their trouble, and he delivered them from their distress; he led them by a straight way, until they reached an inhabited town.
All:	Let them thank the Lord for his steadfast love, for his wonderful works to humankind.
Leader:	Some sat in darkness and in gloom, prisoners in misery and in irons, for they had rebelled against the words of God, and spurned the counsel of the Most High.
Group:	Then they cried to the Lord in their trouble, and he saved them from their distress; he brought them out of darkness and gloom, and broke their bonds asunder.
All:	Let them thank the Lord for his steadfast love, for his wonderful works to humankind.

From Psalm 107

All:	Glory be to him whose power, working in us, can do infinitely more than we can ask or imagine; glory to him from generation to generation in the Church and in Christ Jesus for ever and ever. Amen.

Ephesians 3:20-21

Let us listen carefully to the Word of the Lord,
and attend to it with the ear of our hearts.
Let us welcome it, and faithfully put it into practice.

St. Benedict of Nursia (c.480-c.547) adapted

Explore the Scriptures 2 Corinthians 11:16, 23-27 and 12:7-10

As I have said before, let no one take me for a fool; but if you must, then treat me as a fool and let me do a little boasting of my own. I have worked harder, I have been sent to prison more often, and whipped so many times more, often almost to death. Five times I had the thirty-nine lashes from the Jews; three times I have been beaten with sticks; once I was stoned; three times I have been shipwrecked and once adrift in the open sea for a night and a day. Constantly travelling, I have been in danger from rivers and in danger from brigands, in danger in the open country, danger at sea and danger from so-called brothers. I have worked and laboured, often without sleep; I have been hungry and thirsty and often starving; I have been in the cold without clothes.

To stop me from getting too proud I was given a thorn in the flesh, an angel of Satan to beat me and stop me from getting too proud! About this thing, I have pleaded with the Lord three times for it to leave me, but he has said, 'My grace is enough for you: my power is at its best in weakness'. So I shall be very happy to make my weaknesses my special boast so that the power of Christ may stay over me, and that is why I am quite content with my weaknesses, and with insults, hardships, persecutions, and the agonies I go through for Christ's sake. For it is when I am weak that I am strong.

Following a short period of silence you may wish to share an image, a thought, a phrase that has struck you.

Reflection

What does St. Paul mean when he says 'when I am weak that I am strong'? In a society that prizes self-sufficiency Paul's claim may seem rather strange. We are led to believe that independence and strength are things to be embraced not relinquished. For many, weakness is something to be avoided as it puts us at the mercy of others and can leave us exposed, vulnerable, needy. However, Paul, in his second letter to the Corinthians, speaks of suffering humiliation, disempowerment, bitterness and anger for the sake of Christ. Here Paul seems to be embraces weakness seeing it as an opportunity.

'Offering our living bodies as a holy sacrifice' (Romans 12:1), we are no longer able to model ourselves on the way the world works but our behaviour must change. St. Paul says that such total dedication to God the Father is the only way to 'discover the will of God' for us, to 'know what is the perfect thing to do' (Romans 12:2). When Paul says 'when I am weak that I am strong' it is because he knows that God has power beyond comprehension. Where our knowledge, power or tolerance of suffering fall short, God is ready to make up for any deficiency. God never allows us to take more than we can stand (1 Corinthians 10:13).

In weakness we learn, in a particular way, a lot about the relationship that lies at the heart of our wellbeing; our dependence on God. It may seem easy to turn to God in moments of weakness but do we invite him into our everyday lives? From day to day, when things are 'OK' or 'fine' rather than in a moment of crisis, how conscious am I of my dependence on God?

How have I used weakness as a way of offering something up to God? What weaknesses have helped me to appreciate my dependence upon God? Am I truly candid in my prayer?

Leader: Aloud or in the silence of our hearts let us bring to the Father our thanks (pause)…

Leader: In sorrow let us ask the Father for forgiveness (pause)…

Leader: With confidence let us entrust to the Father our cares and concerns (pause)…

Closing Prayer

Heavenly Father,
open our minds and hearts to the working of your Holy Spirit.
Enlightened by Truth and emboldened through Grace,
may faith overcome doubt, love conquer hatred,
hope shine through suffering,
and zeal mark our proclamation of the Good News
that St. Paul preached to the peoples of all nations.
We ask this through your Son Jesus Christ
who lives and reigns with you, in the unity of the Holy Spirit,
one God for ever and ever.
Amen.

You may wish to take a few moments to ponder another of St. Paul's letters (1 Corinthians 4:1-4, 8-17) in which St. Paul calls the Corinthians, and us, to our senses, criticising self-importance and pride. Here, he talks of the trials we can endure for our faith in the sure knowledge that we can call God, Our Father.

You may also care to reflect (2 Timothy 2:1-13 and Philemon 13).

Read the Scripture from the 30th Sunday in Ordinary Time (Year A) – I Thessalonians 1:5-10

You observed the sort of life we lived when we were with you, which was for your instruction, and you were led to become imitators of us, and of the Lord; and it was with the joy of the Holy Spirit that you took to the gospel, in spite of the great opposition all round you. This has made you the great example to all believers in Macedonia and Achaia since it was from you that the word of the Lord started to spread – and not only throughout Macedonia and Achaia, for the news of your faith in God has spread everywhere. We do not need to tell other people about it: other people tell us how we started the work among you, how you broke with idolatry when you were converted to God and became servants of the real, living God; and how you are now waiting for Jesus, his Son, whom he raised from the dead, to come from heaven to save us from the retribution which is coming.

Background

St. Paul's first letter to the Thessalonians contains several words and expressions that are commonplace to us, but which would have been new to the people of the day. Moreover, old expressions are used in a new way, transformed in meaning by Christ's arrival (see for example Isaiah 52:7 and 61:1). The authors write of 'the gospel' (1:6) and the spreading of 'the word of the Lord' (1:8), phrases related to the missionary proclamation of Jesus Christ, who died, rose from the dead and whose return is awaited. For the Thessalonians, embracing the gospel, the Good News, meant turning (1:9) from idolatry, from cultic religion including Emperor worship, to serve the living God. In this monotheistic faith they received instruction both theologically and ethically (1:6). Having embraced the Christian gospel opposition and suffering (1:7) had to be endured. Their hope of peace and salvation did not rest with the Emperor but with the eternal life offered through sharing in Jesus' Resurrection (1:10). In their imitation of the apostolic ministry as enshrined in the gospel of Jesus (1:6) the faith of the Thessalonians became an example of the Christian life to others in the region (1:8).

Behold me, my beloved Jesus, weighed down
under the burden of my trials and sufferings,
I cast myself at Your feet,
that You may renew my strength and my courage,
while I rest here in Your Presence.
Amen.

make my weaknesses my special boast (2 Corinthians 12:9)

St. Paul leaves us in little doubt that following Christ is a constant challenge, not necessarily of making small adjustments or keeping on an even keel but a life-changing, world-shattering challenge. As it was 2000 years ago, living a life of faith can bring you into conflict with prevailing attitudes (Romans 12:2). Equally challenging is the commonplace assumption that a middle way must be found. Living the Gospel daily is a real challenge, one which we fall short of and may be tempted to run away from.

'Weakness' is essential to living a life of faith. By recognising weakness and vulnerability we can realise that all that burdens us is not ours alone to bear. Weakness is an opportunity to free ourselves from pride, to put ourselves in the hands of another – suffering and weakness stop us short. The ability to be 'weak' is a gift. While striving to be perfect (Philippians 3:12), 'all' is not ours to do. Our weakness, our submission to God, will help us glimpse the way to him.

Alone with none but thee, my God
I journey on my way.
What need I fear, when thou art near
O king of night and day?
More safe am I within thy hand
than if an host didst round me stand.

St. Columba (c.521-597)

let no one take me for a fool (2 Corinthians 11:16)

No one likes to be taken for a fool yet it is all too easy to mock those who passionately express what they feel or believe. We too, may for fear being considered different or foolish neglect to share our opinions, our gifts or our faith. By our words and actions we can exclude people, create outcasts. By our comments and deeds, by ridiculing others we can be the cause of suffering, we can kill a reputation or a person's confidence, offending their dignity. It is perfectly possible to be mocked for being different yet this is precisely what Jesus calls us to do.

During the Sermon on the Mount, Jesus preached a higher standard than the old, he took a commonly accepted rule and went further: 'I have not come to abolish [the Law or the Prophets],' he said 'but to complete them' (Matthew 5:17). Jesus demands that we go one step further, no longer just 'you must not kill' but you must not get angry, call names, you must come to terms with those who offend you. Jesus and Paul, his faithful follower, call us to this higher standard; to go the extra mile in alleviating suffering and anguish and where possible avoiding the circumstances in which it may be caused.

God our Father,
grant that I may rejoice always in hope,
be patient in suffering and
persevere in prayer.
I ask this through your Son, Jesus Christ,
Amen.

Based on Romans 12:12

You may wish to consider joining a small community in your parish for the remainder of this season. If you have not done so already contact your parish priest or a small community leader to explore St. Paul with others in your parish.

The prognosis was not good. I had cancer. I went into hospital for the major operation and felt confused and asked the question 'Why me?' I asked for the Sacrament of the Anointing of the Sick. For me it was a profound experience. It was the Friend of All Friends, Jesus, saying 'Peace'. During the first post-operative weeks complete recovery was uncertain.

The 'time' that is given when a person is diagnosed with cancer is both a challenge and a comfort. Things are never the same again – though that is true of all of us if only we realised it. There is a heightened awareness of the precious nature of time, and of life itself, when living with an intrusive illness. In the Church we speak of 'the grace of the present moment' of time. Each moment is recognised as a gift, precious, to be treasured.

Faith invited a deeper discovery of who and what I was in the sight of God, in the presence of God, beloved by God. I had seen with exceptional clarity that NOTHING, NO-THING can separate me from the love of Jesus Christ. This was, and is being continually confirmed, in the life-giving sacraments of the Church. Knowing that I had been forgiven and am being continually forgiven for having made such a mess of it all - is almost breathtaking! I am witness to these things in a new way. I long for others to share this fundamental consolation. St. Paul's letter to the Romans expresses it so beautifully 'For I am certain of this, neither death nor life...nor any created thing whatever will be able to come between us and the love of God, known to us in Christ Jesus Our Lord' (Romans 8:38).

So, the invitation: If all is going well in my life and I love God that is excellent. If all is going badly in my life and I go on loving God that is even better. That supposes an even greater love.

Sr Amadeus Bulger C

Thanks be to thee, O Lord Jesus Christ,
for all the benefits which thou hast won for us,
for all the pains and insults thou hast borne for us.
O most merciful Redeemer, Friend and Brother,
may I know thee more clearly,
love thee more dearly and
follow thee more nearly day by day.
Amen.

attributed to St Richard of Chichester (1197-1253)

thorn in the flesh (2 Corinthians 12:7)

Suffering is everywhere: from famine or devastation caused by natural disaster to the pain following the loss of a loved one or the suffering caused by illness. While the alleviation of suffering is to be of prime concern, only God is able to eliminate sin, the constant source of suffering (Job 36).

It is possible to see suffering in two ways. Firstly, in suffering there is 'concealed a particular power that draws a person close to Christ, a special grace' (*Salvifici Doloris* or *On the meaning of Human Suffering*, 26). Secondly, the suffering of others permits us to be Christ-like. Pope John Paul II wrote that 'suffering is present in the world in order to release love, in order to give birth to works of love towards neighbour, in order to transform the whole of human civilization into a "civilization of love" '(*On the meaning of Human Suffering*, 30). In suffering there is a chance to unite ourselves with the Cross of Christ to bear our burdens willingly and turn them to God's advantage as witness to the world.

From Spe Salvi (In hope we are saved)

36. Like action, suffering is a part of our human existence. Suffering stems partly from our finitude (our limited time on earth), and partly from the mass of sin which has accumulated over the course of history, and continues to grow unabated today. Certainly we must do whatever we can to reduce suffering: to avoid as far as possible the suffering of the innocent; to soothe pain; to give assistance in overcoming mental suffering. These are obligations both in justice and in love, and they are included among the fundamental requirements of the Christian life and every truly human life... Indeed, we must do all we can to overcome suffering, but to banish it from the world altogether is not in our power... We know that God exists, and hence that this power to 'take

away the sin of the world' (John 1:29) is present in the world. Through faith in the existence of this power, hope for the world's healing has emerged in history.

Give me, good Lord, a full faith, a firm hope and a fervent charity,
a love to thee incomparable above the love to myself.
Give me, good Lord, a longing to be with thee,
not for the avoiding of the calamities of this world,
nor so much for the attaining of the joys of heaven,
as for the very love of thee.
Amen.

St. Thomas More (1478-1535)

Constantly travelling (2 Corinthians 11:26)

Life is made up of many journeys and is in a very real sense a journey itself. We are 'constantly travelling', following the Good Shepherd, confident that he will show us, indeed has shown us by his words and actions, the way to the Father (John 10:1-10; John 14:1-12). The memorial acclamation 'Christ has died, Christ is Risen, Christ will come again' expresses this, it is a shout of joy as we remember what God has done for us, a reminder of Christ's triumph over death. The sufferings and hardships we endure, he has endured. Death which will greet each of us, greeted him. Jesus' resurrection from the dead, we hope to share (Philippians 3:10-11).

At last, all-powerful Master,
you give leave to your servant
to go in peace, according to your promise.
For my eyes have seen your salvation,
which you have prepared for all nations,
the light to enlighten the Gentiles,
and give glory to Israel, your people.
Amen.

Nunc Dimittis (or Song of Simeon, Luke 2:29-32

Addressing the people and his disciples Jesus said, 'The scribes and the Pharisees occupy the chair of Moses. You must therefore do what they tell you and listen to what they say; but do not be guided by what they do: since they do not practise what they preach. They tie up heavy burdens and lay them on men's shoulders, but will they lift a finger to move them? Not they! Everything they do is done to attract attention, like wearing broader phylacteries and longer tassels, like wanting to take the place of honour at banquets and the front seats in the synagogues, being greeted obsequiously in the market squares and having people call them Rabbi.

You, however, must not allow yourselves to be called Rabbi, since you have only one Master, and you are all brothers and sisters. You must call no one on earth your father, since you have only one Father, and he is in heaven. Nor must you allow yourselves to be called teachers, for you have only one Teacher, the Christ. The greatest among you must be your servant. Anyone who exalts himself will be humbled, and anyone who humbles himself will be exalted.'

Matthew 23:1-12

We are often called to 'blow our own trumpet' and to shout of our successes and skills. Where can we find the opportunity to demonstrate humility for Christ and before each other?

O blessed Jesus,
give me stillness of soul in you.
Let your mighty calmness reign in me.
Rule me, O King of Gentleness,
King of Peace.

St. John of the Cross (1542-1591)

It is easy to conceive of St. Paul's journeys much as we would a holiday; thinking that the route, the stops, the accommodation and visits were all pre-planned. However, no-one had been an evangelist in this way before and there was no model to follow. When Paul had been in Jerusalem, he started out on what we loosely call his 'missionary journeys'. But they were not journeys in the normal sense of the word. He didn't seem to have any particular plan for which community he would visit next; no fixed itinerary. He relied on the inspiration of the Spirit which does appear to have been a clear and identifiable force in his life. He had no particular project in mind; how long his journey would last or how many communities would be included in his visits. For example, it seems he lived for some two years in Corinth, until he felt the need to move on.

The 'journeys' took him around most of the Eastern Mediterranean, where he preached in Cyprus and southern Galatia (1st journey). From Antioch he revisited the Churches in Galatia and then on to Asia and Macedonia and Achaia before returning to Jerusalem via Corinth (2nd journey).

Much of Paul's work involved revisiting churches he had previously founded such as the one at Ephesus were he stayed for over two years. When he could not visit he wrote. Paul's third 'journey' took him back to Jerusalem (3rd journey) with money for the 'Christian' community there, much as we have a collection on Good Friday for the Holy Places. His final 'journey', that to Rome, led eventually to his death.

See the map of St. Paul's journeys in the pull-out at the back of the booklet.

Opening Prayer

Leader:	O Lord, you have searched me and known me. You know when I sit down and when I rise up; you discern my thoughts from far away.
Group:	Where can I go from your spirit? Or where can I flee from your presence?
Leader:	If I ascend to heaven, you are there; If I take the wings of the morning and settle at the farthest limits of the sea, even there your hand shall lead me.
Group:	For it was you who formed my inward parts; you knit me together in my mother's womb. I praise you, for I am fearfully and wonderfully made. Wonderful are your works; that I know very well.
Leader:	How weighty are your thoughts, O God!

From Psalm 139

All: Glory be to him whose power, working in us, can do infinitely more than we can ask or imagine; glory to him from generation to generation in the Church and in Christ Jesus for ever and ever. Amen.

Ephesians 3:20-21

Let us listen carefully to the Word of the Lord,
and attend to it with the ear of our hearts.
Let us welcome it, and faithfully put it into practice.

St. Benedict of Nursia (c.480-c.547) adapted

Explore the Scriptures Ephesians 3:8-21

I, who am less than the least of all the saints, have been entrusted with this special grace, not only of proclaiming to the pagans the infinite treasure of Christ but also of explaining how the mystery is to be dispensed. Through all the ages, this has been kept hidden in God, the creator of everything. Why? So that the Sovereignties and Powers should learn only now, through the Church, how comprehensive God's wisdom really is, exactly according to the plan which he had had from all eternity in Christ Jesus our Lord. This is why we are bold enough to approach God in complete confidence, through our faith in him; so, I beg you, never lose confidence just because of the trials that I go through on your account: they are your glory.

This then, is what I pray, kneeling before the Father, from whom every family, whether spiritual or natural, takes its name:

Out of his infinite glory, may he give you the power through his Spirit for your hidden self to grow strong, so that Christ may live in your hearts through faith, and then, planted in love and built on love, you will with all the saints have strength to grasp the breadth and the length, the height and the depth; until, knowing the love of Christ, which is beyond all knowledge, you are filled with the utter fullness of God.

Glory be to him whose power, working in us, can do infinitely more than we can ask or imagine; glory to him from generation to generation in the Church and in Christ Jesus for ever and ever. Amen.

Following a short period of silence you may wish to share an image, a thought, a phrase that has struck you.

Reflection

In the course of his early years, St. Paul learned his trade as a tentmaker. He went on to complete his studies to be a rabbi while living in Jerusalem. Clearly, he had ample opportunities to develop his intellectual gifts. Today, with the onset of the Internet and other technological advances, there is little that we cannot investigate and learn about to satisfy our own quest for knowledge. Given the extent of these resources, some may doubt that there are matters beyond human comprehension. Yet, to be a person of faith is to accept what cannot be fully explained by scientific discovery or human perception. In other words, God cannot be succinctly defined by any rationale no matter how brilliant or by any expression no matter how pious. By not fully knowing or completely understanding, we are drawn into the mystery - to ponder again and again God's plan for our salvation, which he has chosen to reveal to us through his Son, Christ Jesus.

St. Paul did not see Christ's earthly ministry first hand. Nor did he initially grasp Christ's message. However, St. Paul's perspective of the world was challenged, on the road to Damascus, when he encountered the Risen Lord. Temporarily blinded by the brightness of the light, Paul accepted God's loving invitation and began 'to walk by faith not by sight' (2 Corinthians 5:7). While our own experience may not have been quite as dramatic, the same life-changing invitation has been given to each of us. Washed clean in baptismal waters and wrapped in a white garment, we were transformed and made 'one with Christ' (Ephesians 2:11-22). This transformation, our having been 'made righteous by faith with Christ', (Galatians 4:5-7) at our own baptisms may have happened quite sometime ago, yet, each year at the Easter Vigil we have an opportunity to re-live this life-giving moment and resolve yet again to model Christ in our daily living - to walk by faith not by sight.

St. Paul reminds us that the practice of our faith is nourished in the Church, the visible Body of Christ. Each time we gather to celebrate the Eucharist we enter into the great mystery that is our faith. In the sacraments visible signs help us to contemplate the invisible, our life 'in Christ'. This life in Christ is a wondrous gift of the Father which 'entitles each of us to say the prayer of the children of God: "Our Father" (*Catechism of the Catholic Church, 1243*).

It is often easy to follow the wisdom of the world than to live 'in Christ'. Where in your life are you being invited to 'walk in faith not by sight'? What event or person has helped you to a greater understanding of the mystery of faith?

Leader: Aloud or in the silence of our hearts let us bring to the Father our thanks (pause)…

Leader: In sorrow let us ask the Father for forgiveness (pause)…

Leader: With confidence let us entrust to the Father our cares and concerns (pause)…

Closing Prayer

Heavenly Father,
open our minds and hearts to the working of your Holy Spirit.
Enlightened by Truth and emboldened through Grace,
may faith overcome doubt, love conquer hatred,
hope shine through suffering,
and zeal mark our proclamation of the Good News
that St. Paul preached to the peoples of all nations.
We ask this through your Son Jesus Christ
who lives and reigns with you, in the unity of the Holy Spirit,
one God for ever and ever.
Amen.

You may also want to look at (Colossians 2:9-10) in which Paul tells us where we can find fulfilment. The life, death and resurrection of Christ is a gift without parallel, one we often find hard to grasp but believe through faith. Reflect on (Romans 5:6-15) and (Galatians 3:23-29) in this light.

Read the Scripture from All Saints' Day - I John 3:1-3

Think of the love that the Father has lavished on us, by letting us be called God's children; and that is what we are. Because the world refused to acknowledge him, therefore it does not acknowledge us. My dear people, we are already the children of God but what we are to be in the future has not yet been revealed; all we know is, that when it is revealed we shall be like him because we shall see him as he really is. Surely everyone who entertains this hope must purify himself, must try to be as pure as Christ.

Background

As we have learned, St. Paul frequently engaged in letter writing to convey the message of God to specific communities. Although the author of I John does not use the same letter writing formula, he and St. Paul sent words of encouragement to challenge and guide the early Christians when they could not be with them. For the most part, the themes were similar in that they both wrote about the implications of becoming one of God's children (I John 3:1; Romans 5:5), the difficulties of living in imitation of Christ in a world that continually challenges these values (I John 2:15; John 15:17-19; Romans 13:8), and the promise of the eternal life given at baptism and glimpsed here on earth (I John 3:2; Philippians 3:14).

Father, all powerful and ever-ling God,
today we rejoice in the holy men and women of every time and place.
May their prayers bring us your forgiveness and love.
We ask this through Jesus Christ, your Son,
who lives and reigns with you and the Holy Spirit,
one God, for ever and ever.
Amen.

Opening Prayer, Solemnity of All Saints, Roman Missal (1974)

All the Saints (Ephesians 3:8)

For centuries the Church has looked upon the saints as intercessors; there to intercede on our behalf or help us in our prayerful petitions to God, our Father. During his papacy, Pope John Paul II encouraged us to look to the saints as role models – examples of how we might live in the likeness of Christ. Having canonised more saints (over 450) than all of his predecessors combined, Pope John Paul II gave us a number of twentieth century saints. These included young persons, married men and women as well as religious. Regardless of their particular vocation the saints can be looked upon as inspiration for daily living. Whatever trials and difficulties they encountered during their earthly lives, the saints offered them to God – just as St. Paul instructed when he wrote to the Corinthians, 'whatever you do, do it for the glory of God' (1 Corinthians 10:31). Through our baptism, we are called to do the same – to imitate the saints.

Most days, the Church honours a particular saint for whom information abounds in books, newspapers and via the Internet (for example http://americancatholic.org/Features/SaintofDay/default.asp). Perhaps the life of a saint could become a part of your walk-to-school or dinner-time conversation.

God of all holiness,
you gave your saints different gifts on earth
but one reward in heaven.
May the prayers of the saints be our constant encouragement
and may we, with the faithful departed we commemorate today,
share the joys and blessings of the life to come.
We ask this through Jesus Christ, your Son,
who lives and reigns with you and the Holy Spirit,
one God, for ever and ever.
Amen.

Adapted from the Opening Prayers for All Saints and All Souls, Roman Missal (1974)

kneeling before the Father... (Ephesians 3:14)

Gestures such as kneeling, standing and processing enable us to actively participate in the Eucharist. Most importantly, they are intended help us set aside our earthly thoughts and endeavours so that we can turn our minds and hearts to God our Father. Similarly, on entering a church, we dip our figures in holy water and make the Sign of the Cross as a reminder of our baptism and our life 'in Christ'. By this gesture, we not only recall His death on the cross, we affirm our own dying with him. As St. Paul explained to the Galatians: 'I have been crucified with Christ; it is no longer I who live, but Christ lives in me; and the life which I now live in the flesh I live by faith in the Son of God, who loved me and gave Himself for me' (Galatians 2:20).

May Christ's words be in my mind,
on my lips, and in my heart.

Prayer to accompany the signing of the forehead, the lips
and the breast before the gospel reading

I'm over 21 (by a number of years), was born into a Catholic family in Bedfordshire, and am the youngest of five children. Faith was an important part of our family life and in addition to Sunday Mass attendance, bedtime prayers were part and parcel of my childhood routine.

I suppose my faith didn't really become my own until my late teenage years. Going to Church and saying my prayers were something I did, but I wouldn't have said I had a deep personal relationship with Jesus, that came later. Going to University marked a real turning point in my faith. It was here that I joined a weekly parish prayer group and discovered a fellowship that I'd not found before. The people there were really sincere about their faith. They wanted to learn more about Jesus and the Bible and that rubbed off on me in a powerful way.

I began to read the Bible on my own. I began to pray more, spending quiet time before Jesus in the Blessed Sacrament. Gradually my Catholic faith and my relationship with Jesus developed. Life has not always been easy. My father died when I was six, others dear to me have since died, and members of my own family have been struck down with serious illnesses and tragedies. I can say that my faith has carried me through these times. Hand on heart I can truly say that my faith brings me deep happiness and fulfilment which I can't find in anything else.

Clare Ward

Lord, make me an instrument of your peace;
where there is hatred, let me sow love;
when there is injury, pardon;
where there is doubt, faith;
where there is despair, hope;
where there is darkness, light;
and where there is sadness, joy.
Amen.

The Peace Prayer attributed to St. Francis of Assisi (c.1181-1226)

planted in love and built on love (Ephesians 3:17)

By our baptism we are lovingly joined with Christ in his death and resurrection to become 'a new creation' (Galatians 6:15, 2 Corinthians 5:17). Baptism is clearly more than just a welcome into the Church or a reason for a social celebration. Here, a new life gifted by God is presented to him as the parents seek, for their child, an opportunity to share eternal life with Christ. From that moment, through the love of God, our earthly life's goal is planted in our hearts. All new life needs nourishment. Parents, as primary educators of their children, are called to build a spiritual home – a place where their witness to God's love will enable their children to grow in faith and love for one another. As a sign of this undertaking, to keep the 'flame of faith alive', parents and godparents are given a lighted candle.

Father in heaven,
the light of your revelation brought Paul
the gift of faith in Jesus your Son.
Through his prayers
may we always give thanks for your life
given us in Christ Jesus,
and for having been enriched by him
in all knowledge and love.
We ask this through Christ our Lord.
Amen.

Alternative Opening Prayer, Vigil Mass
of SS Peter and Paul, Roman Missal (adapted)

Glory to him... (Ephesians 3:20)

The word 'doxology' may not be a familiar term yet these prayers of praise are an integral part of the practice of the Catholic faith. Besides the Glory Be that is said at the end of each decade of the Rosary, there are other well known doxologies including the Gloria that is said during the celebration of Holy Mass. Using a Jewish tradition, St. Paul included several doxologies in his writings to early Christians to give praise to God our Father (cf. Romans 11: 36, Galatians 1:5).

All too easily our personal prayer can become a cycle of petition and thanksgiving – asking God for special favours and thanking him on their receipt. For sure, God invites us to seek his help, yet prayer is not akin to bargaining or a matter of negotiation. Christ himself taught us to pray that our wills be moulded to the will of the Father – thy will be done on earth as it is in heaven.

Have our prayers become a rather hollow recitation of words or an opportunity for loving praise of God's greatness – secure in the knowledge that each of us has been offered the gift of eternal salvation?

Glory be to him who can keep you from falling
and bring you safe to his glorious presence,
innocent and happy.
To God, the only God,
who saves us through Jesus Christ our Lord,
be the glory, majesty, authority and power,
which he had before time began,
now and forever.
Amen.

Doxology from the Letter of Jude 24-25

Jesus told this parable to his disciples: 'The kingdom of heaven will be like this: Ten bridesmaids took their lamps and went to meet the bridegroom. Five of them were foolish and five were sensible: the foolish ones did take their lamps, but they brought no oil, whereas the sensible ones took flasks of oil as well as their lamps. The bridegroom was late, and they all grew drowsy and fell asleep. But at midnight there was a cry, "The bridegroom is here! Go out and meet him." At this, all those bridesmaids woke up and trimmed their lamps, and the foolish ones said to the sensible ones, "Give us some of your oil: our lamps are going out." But they replied, "There may not be enough for us and for you; you had better go to those who sell it and buy some for yourselves." They had gone off to buy it when the bridegroom arrived. Those who were ready went in with him to the wedding hall and the door was closed. The other bridesmaids arrived later. "Lord, Lord," they said "open the door for us." But he replied, "I tell you solemnly, I do not know you." So stay awake, because you do not know either the day or the hour.'

Matthew 25:1-13

It is natural to put of until tomorrow what ought to be done today. The five foolish bridesmaids were caught off guard having no spare oil. Our preparations for Christmas may well be underway; we may even have the presents bought, cards written and a date for picking up the turkey. This reading is a call to action, an opportunity to start doing what needs to be done to prepare ourselves for Christ's coming again in glory.

God, you reveal your glory in the life and in the power of your Risen Son.
We pray that your Kingdom will come.
We long for the glorious day of Christ's revelation
when the kingdom of death and tears will end
and your kingdom of peace, justice and love will be established forever.
Amen.

Prayer by Ethiopian Orthodox during Week of Prayer
for Christian Unity 2004 in Jerusalem

Paul and the place of scripture

'Let the Word of Christ, in all its richness, find a home in you' *(Colossians 3:16).*

Scripture is the 'truth which God wished to be set down… for the sake of our salvation' (Dei Verbum, 11), 'acting in' and 'through' sacred writers such as St. Paul. At the time of St. Paul's writing the Canon of Scripture (what is included in the Bible) had not been decided upon. Indeed, St. Paul's letters which teach what had been revealed by God through the life of Christ and handed on by the Apostles, constitute the earliest pieces of the New Testament, written before the Gospels. For Paul and the other Apostles, the important thing was for communities and believers to hold on to the apostolic traditions being handed on by word of mouth or by letter (cf. 2 Thessalonians 2:15). While some of these oral teachings were eventually written down and now form Holy Scripture, other teachings such as the number of sacraments and the Assumption of Mary come to us in the form of Sacred Tradition (Latin tradere – to hand on). Both are equally authoritative and together form the 'Sacred deposit' of the faith.

The Pope together with the bishops of the Church have a teaching authority (Magisterium) and are tasked with giving an authentic interpretation of the Word of God, whether in its written form or in the form of Tradition (CCC, 85). It is important to understand each passage of Scripture in the harmony and coherence of all the truths of faith (Dei Verbum, 12) making constant reference to the Tradition and teaching authority of the Church. 'In accord with God's most wise design, Sacred Tradition, Holy Scripture and the Magisterium are so linked and joined together that one cannot stand without the others… all together and each in its own way under the action of the one Holy Spirit contribute effectively to the salvation of souls' (Dei Verbum, 10).

St. Paul recognised that Jesus' life, death and resurrection fulfilled the promises of the Old Testament. Together the Old and New Testaments demonstrate the unity of God's plan and his Revelation. It is this unity which we speak of when we say that all Sacred Scripture is but one book, and that one book is Christ, because all divine Scripture speaks of Christ, and all divine Scripture is fulfilled in Christ (CCC, 134).

Opening Prayer

Leader: The voice of the Lord is over the waters;
the God of glory thunders,
the Lord, over mighty waters.

Group: The voice of the Lord is powerful;
the voice of the Lord is full of majesty.

Leader: The voice of the Lord flashes forth flames of fire.
The voice of the Lord shakes the wilderness;
the Lord shakes the wilderness of Kadesh.

Group: The Lord sits enthroned over the flood;
the Lord sits enthroned as king for ever.

Leader: May the Lord give strength to his people!
May the Lord bless his people with peace!

From Psalm 29

All: Glory be to him whose power, working in us, can do
infinitely more than we can ask or imagine; glory to
him from generation to generation in the Church
and in Christ Jesus for ever and ever. Amen.

Ephesians 3:20-21

*Let us listen carefully to the Word of the Lord,
and attend to it with the ear of our hearts.
Let us welcome it, and faithfully put it into practice.*

St. Benedict of Nursia (c.480-c.547) adapted

Explore the Scriptures I Corinthians 12:12-31

Just as a human body, though it is made up of many parts, is a single unit because all these parts, though many, make one body, so it is with Christ. In the one Spirit we were all baptised, Jews as well as Greeks, slaves as well as citizens, and one Spirit was given to us all to drink. Nor is the body to be identified with any one of its many parts. If the foot were to say, 'I am not a hand and so I do not belong to the body', would that mean that it stopped being part of the body? If the ear were to say, 'I am not an eye, and so I do not belong to the body', would that mean that it was not a part of the body? If your whole body was just one eye, how would you hear anything? If it was just one ear, how would you smell anything?

Instead of that, God put all the separate parts into the body on purpose. If all the parts were the same, how could it be a body? As it is, the parts are many but the body is one. The eye cannot say to the hand, 'I do not need you', nor can the head say to the feet, 'I do not need you'. What is more, it is precisely the parts of the body that seem to be the weakest which are the indispensable ones; and it is the least honourable parts of the body that we clothe with the greatest care. So our more improper parts get decorated in a way that our more proper parts do not need. God has arranged the body so that more dignity is given to the parts which are without it, and so that there may not be disagreements inside the body, but that each part may be equally concerned for all the others. If one part is hurt, all parts are hurt with it. If one part is given special honour, all parts enjoy it. Now you together are Christ's body; but each of you is a different part of it. In the Church, God has given the first place to apostles, the second to prophets, the third to teachers; after them, miracles, and after them the gift of healing; helpers, good leaders, those with many languages. Are all of them apostles, or all of them prophets, or all of them teachers? Do they all have the gift of miracles or all have the gift of healing? Do all speak strange languages, and all interpret them? Be ambitious for the higher gifts. And I am going to show you a way that is better than any of them.

Following a short period of silence you may wish to share an image, a thought, a phrase that has struck you.

Reflection

With such a familiar reading, it is hard to imagine that anything new can be said. This passage is frequently used in confirmation preparation, it has been used to prepare groups for parish leadership and we hear it every year at Pentecost. Its familiarity, however, lies in the fact that we hear echoes of its message in daily life as a Christian. We all search for a role, consciously or subconsciously, whether it is in our families, the workplace, in a group of friends or in the Church. The desire to belong and feel needed is a strong motivator. It is not surprising that the image of the family is particularly strong when referring to the Church. Everywhere in the New Testament and particularly in St. Paul's letters, the Church is described as being composed of women and men united as sisters and brothers in one family. 'The Spirit himself and our spirit bear united witness that we are the children of God. And if we are children we are heirs as well: heirs of God and coheirs with Christ, sharing his sufferings so as to share in his glory' (Romans 8:16-17).

St. Paul created communities throughout the Mediterranean, places where experiences could be shared, bread broken and Scripture heard and lived out. Where Roman gods demanded individual responsibility for the offering of sacrifice and oblation, this new faith in Christ was manifested in community. Catholic Christianity was, is, a personal relationship with God grounded in the Church as the Second Vatican Council's Dogmatic Constitution on the Church tells us:

God does not make men holy and save them merely as individuals, without bond or link between one another… Christ instituted [a] new covenant, in His Blood, calling together a people made up of Jew and Gentile, making them one, not according to the flesh but in the Spirit. This was to be the new People of God… Established by Christ as a communion of life, charity and truth, it is also used by Him as an instrument for the redemption of all, and is sent forth into the whole world as the light of the world and the salt of the earth (*Lumen Gentium*, 9).

What distinguished the communities of the early Church was the shared belief in the saving power and the love of God incarnate in Jesus Christ. Such love should characterise our parishes, our families, our communities. St. Paul asks us to 'put on love' (Colossians 3:14). This love is to serve both those present in the community and to act as a beacon to those around it, calling them to itself. St. Augustine sums this up beautifully in one of his sermons: 'We ourselves are the house of God. By becoming Christians we are like stones newly quarried and when catechised, baptised, formed we are hewn and evened up.' Nevertheless, Augustine continued, we 'do not make the house of God unless we are cemented together by love. It is only when people see that the stones and wood in the building are securely fastened to each other that they would enter without fear of collapse'.

At what point did you feel that you 'belonged' to your parish? How has your experience of a small community helped you to 'belong'? How might you, as individuals and as a group, help others feel a sense of 'belonging'? Do we see our gifts as personal possessions or as something to be used for the good of our community?

Leader: Aloud or in the silence of our hearts let us bring to the Father our thanks (pause)…

Leader: In sorrow let us ask the Father for forgiveness (pause)…

Leader: With confidence let us entrust to the Father our cares and concerns (pause)…

Closing Prayer

Heavenly Father,
open our minds and hearts to the working of your Holy Spirit.
Enlightened by Truth and emboldened through Grace,
may faith overcome doubt, love conquer hatred,
hope shine through suffering,
and zeal mark our proclamation of the Good News
that St. Paul preached to the peoples of all nations.
We ask this through your Son Jesus Christ
who lives and reigns with you, in the unity of the Holy Spirit,
one God for ever and ever.
Amen.

Should you have the time you may wish to look at (Colossians 1:15-20 and 25), which focuses on the power and majesty of Christ, the head of all creation, and how as members of the Church we are able to share in God's message. (1 Timothy 3:14-16) and (1 Thessalonians 5:14-18) may also be helpful.

Read the Scripture from The Dedication of the Lateran Basilica - 1 Corinthians 3: 9-11, 16-17

You are God's building. By the grace God gave me, I succeeded as an architect and laid the foundations, on which someone else is doing the building. Everyone doing the building must work carefully. For the foundation, nobody can lay any other than the one which has already been laid, that is Jesus Christ. Didn't you realise that you were God's temple and that the Spirit of God was living among you? If anybody should destroy the temple of God, God will destroy him, because the temple of God is sacred; and you are that temple.

Background

St. Paul had an uneasy relationship with the church of Corinth. He detected disunity amongst its members (1 Corinthians 1:11-13), discontent with his apostolic ministry (2 Corinthians 10:7-12), difficulties in understanding the effects of the salvation wrought through Christ as a result of his death and resurrection (1 Cor. 15:12-14) and an inability on the part of some church members to reflect Christian values in society (1 Cor. 5:1-2; 6:17-20).

'God's building' (1 Cor. 3:9) is a reference to the Christian community, who in Paul's time would have met in the houses of its members. As a result terms like 'building', 'foundations' and 'architect' become metaphors for how the Church ought to be perceived (1 Cor. 3:10b), of its relationship to its apostolic founder, Paul (1 Cor. 3:10a) and of the necessity of viewing the whole structure as being based on the mission and ministry of Jesus Christ (1 Cor. 3:11). Paul is offering a challenge to the church leaders in Corinth to remain faithful to the Gospel which he has preached (1 Cor. 15:3-4) and to the testimony of the earliest eye-witnesses of Jesus' resurrection.

Paul also uses another metaphor for the church, that of 'God's Temple' which contains 'God's Spirit' (1 Cor. 3:16-17). The physical body of the Christian should be regarded as 'a temple of the Holy Spirit' (1 Cor. 6:19). It is likely that Paul is reflecting upon the role and purpose of the Jerusalem Temple which was believed to be the dwelling place of God on earth (1 Kings 8:12-13). In using this metaphor Paul is making a direct link between the status of the Church and the ethical behaviour expected of Christians.

God our Father,
from living stones, your chosen people,
you built an eternal temple to your glory.
Increase the spiritual gifts you have given to your Church,
so that your faithful people may continue to grow
into the new and eternal Jerusalem.
We ask this through our Lord Jesus Christ, your Son,
Who lives and reigns with you and the Holy Spirit,
One God, for ever and ever.
Amen.

Opening Prayer, Dedication of a Church, Roman Missal (1974)

In the one Spirit we were all baptised (1 Corinthians 12:13)

Through baptism we enter into communion with Christ's death, are buried with him, and rise with him (Romans 6:3-4, cf. Colossians 2:12). The baptised, reborn in the Holy Spirit (Acts 2:38, John 3:5), become 'living stones' incorporated into the 'spiritual house' of the Church (*Catechism*, 1267).

Thirty to forty years ago the parish community was all important. Important events, moments of transition, were experienced and marked within the 'spiritual house' of the faith community. Increasingly though, religion is seen as a private or individualistic affair. Moreover, the commitment to the parish community has to take its place alongside the other demands on our time.

For St. Paul community was everything. Throughout his letters we see a concern to build up the community through a unity of belief and through fellowship. For Paul the building of *communio* is the antidote to loneliness and isolation. In community the weak are strengthened, anonymity challenged and genuine love and welcome become possible.

From Apostolicam Actuositatem

10. In the manner of the men and women who helped Paul in spreading the Gospel (cf. Acts 18:18, 26; Romans 16:3) the laity with the right apostolic attitude supply what is lacking to their brethren and refresh the spirit of pastors and of the rest of the faithful (cf. 1 Corinthians 16:17-18). Strengthened by active participation in the liturgical life of their community, they are eager to do their share of the apostolic works of that community. They bring to the Church people who perhaps are far removed from it, earnestly cooperate in presenting the word of God... and offer their special skills to make the care of souls... more efficient and effective.

We believe in one holy, catholic and apostolic Church.
We acknowledge one baptism for the forgiveness of sins.
We look for the resurrection of the dead,
and the life of the word to come.
Amen.

Part of the Profession of Faith

the parts are many but the body is one (1 Corinthians 12:20)

How can we be Christians in the modern world? How can we live Christian lives in societies caricatured as soulless and self-serving? These are not trick questions. God has given us the means of living as believers in a troublesome world. We have the Church, the sacraments and the outpouring of the Holy Spirit. All these are given to strengthen us. In addition we have the example and support of each other. St. Paul, in his first letter to the Church in Thessalonica, wrote: 'You observed the sort of life we lived, you were led to become imitators of us, you took to the gospel, from you the Word of God started to spread, news of your faith has spread everywhere' (1 Thessalonians 1:5-8). Our example to those around us, in our parish community, makes it easier for them to bear the joyful burden of Christian and Eucharistic living. Likewise, their example supports us.

From Apostolicam Actuositatem

10. The parish offers an obvious example of the apostolate on the community level inasmuch as it brings together the many human differences within its boundaries and merges them into the universality of the Church. The laity should accustom themselves to working in the parish in union with their priests, bringing to the Church community their own and the world's problems as well as questions concerning human salvation, all of which they should examine and resolve by deliberating in common. As far as possible the laity ought to provide helpful collaboration for every apostolic and missionary undertaking sponsored by their local parish.

God our Father,
by the promise you made
in the life, death, and resurrection of Christ your Son,
you bring together in your Spirit, from all the nations,
a people to be your own.
Keep the Church faithful to its mission:
may it be a leaven in the world
renewing us in Christ,
and transforming us into your family.
Amen.

Opening Prayer, Mass for the Universal Church, Roman Missal (1974)

I would like to share with you how I came to know Jesus Christ. It wasn't necessarily a dramatic encounter, but rather a step by step journey. However, even if the encounter wasn't dramatic, the changes in my life have been. I wasn't brought up a Christian at all, but for some reason at the age of about fourteen I started going to my local sleepy Anglican parish. Shortly after, there was a Billy Graham mission in the parish and a call for those who wanted to give their lives to Jesus. I went forward. If God had been scripting a Hollywood film, then this would have been the cue for a dramatic life changing moment. Instead, seemingly, nothing altered in my life.

A few years later I went to university in Bristol. Here I met a Jehovah's Witness, who awoke in me a desire to find God and to find the truth. We studied Scripture together and I became hungry to discover more. I was lead by some Christians to a course, similar to Alpha, at an evangelical Anglican church. Here it all made sense. Here I came to see that God is real, God is alive and my life meant nothing without Him. I met Jesus as my Lord, King, Saviour, brother and friend.

Now that could be the end but meeting Jesus was only the beginning. I was a believer, but Jesus had two further extremely vital encounters for me. Firstly, He showed me the Holy Spirit, who made my faith alive and active by taking it the incredibly long distance from the mind to the heart. Secondly, He introduced me to Christian community. In Poland, I met Koinonia John the Baptist, which is an international charismatic Catholic community. This was a life-changing experience. Praise the Lord, I didn't meet either the Church or the community as an organisation but as people who are alive in Christ and gave witness to Jesus' resurrection in their lives. It is not possible to overstate how important Christian community is.

Michael Parr

Living God, we praise you for the multitudes of women,
men, young people and children who, across the earth,
are striving to be witnesses to peace,
to trust and to reconciliation.
Amen.

Taizé prayer, Time of the Church I

the weakest which are the indispensable ones (1 Corinthians 12:22)

Welcome and inclusivity are not optional extras to parish life. The parish is a sacred space where we are able to live out our baptismal vocation, to act on the call to minister to one another and provide witness to the world. The notion of mutual support and the need for prayer are imperative to the proper functioning of a parish and to a healthy life as one of God's children.

During the 'I Confess', each Sunday we pray the following: 'I ask blessed Mary, ever virgin, all the angels and saints, and you, my brothers and sisters, to pray for me to the Lord our God.' In this we are not simply asking for help but pledging our support to those around us. We acknowledge the importance that each part of the Church's body plays and assert that each part be equally concerned for all the others (cf. Romans 15:1-6).

If we look to the 'margins' of our community, who do we see? Who are the 'weakest' in our community? How can we facilitate their involvement?

Father,
look with love on those you have called
to share in the one sacrifice of Christ.
By the power of the Holy Spirit
make them one body, healed of all division.
Keep us all in communion of mind and heart,
and help us to work together
for the coming of your kingdom.
Amen.

From the Eucharistic Prayer for Reconciliation I

If you have not done so already, there may still be an opportunity to join a small community in which you can pray and share your faith.

Set your mind on the higher gifts (1 Corinthians 12:31)

'Greater love hath no man, than to lay down his life for his friends' (John 15:13). The shedding of Christ's blood on Calvary is a gift beyond compare, a sacrifice which makes all others redundant (Hebrews 10:12) It is possible, in the midst of the here and now, in the sacrifice of the Mass to see once more this great act of God's love. Rightly described as the source and summit of Christian life (*Lumen Gentium*, 11), the Eucharist feeds us for life, it is the source from which we spring, it too is the place where we can outpour our thanks and love to the Father for the gift of grace though his Son.

We are told by Paul to seek grace, that strength which comes from God, before concerning ourselves with gifts; but where we aspire to gifts, to look to those which are the most valuable in themselves or the most serviceable to others. Set our minds on the higher gifts, and by their use, by example and word, inspire and convince others of the beauty and greatness of God.

From Christifideles Laici (Lay Members of Christ's Faithful People)

36. Communion and mission are profoundly connected with each other, they interpenetrate and mutually imply each other, to the point that communion represents both the source and the fruit of mission: communion gives rise to mission and mission is accomplished in communion. It is always the one and the same Spirit who calls together and unifies the Church and sends her to preach the Gospel 'to the ends of the earth' (Acts 1:8).

Lord Jesus Christ,
help us go forward in hope!
Relying on your help as we venture upon
the vast ocean of this new millennium
help us not to rely on our efforts alone
but to believe in the grace of God the Father,
and the assurance of your presence amongst us.
Amen.

From Communion and Mission: Pastoral Priorities for the Dioce
of Westminster, adapte

Jesus spoke this parable to his disciples: 'The kingdom of heaven is like a man on his way abroad who summoned his servants and entrusted his property to them. To one he gave five talents, to another two, to a third one; each in proportion to his ability. Then he set out.

The man who had received the five talents promptly went and traded with them and made five more. The man who had received two made two more in the same way. But the man who had received one went off and dug a hole in the ground and hid his master's money.

Now a long time after, the master of those servants came back and went through his accounts with them. The man who had received the five talents came forward bringing five more. "Sir," he said, "you entrusted me with five talents; here are five more that I have made."

His master said to him, "Well done, good and faithful servant; you have shown you can be faithful in small things, I will trust you with greater; come and join in your master's happiness." Next the man with two talents came forward. "Sir," he said, "you entrusted me with two talents; here are two more that I have made." His master said to him, "Well done, good and faithful servant; you have shown you can be faithful in small things, I will trust you with greater; come and join in your master's happiness." Last came forward the man who had the one talent. "Sir," said he, "I had heard you were a hard man, reaping where you have not sown and gathering where you have not scattered; so I was afraid, and I went off and hid your talent in the ground. Here it is; it was yours, you have it back." But his master answered him, "You wicked and lazy servant! So you knew that I reap where I have not sown and gather where I have not scattered? Well then, you should have deposited my money with the bankers, and on my return I would have recovered my capital with interest.

So now, take the talent from him and give it to the man who has the five talents. For to everyone who has will be given more, and he will have more than enough; but from the man who has not, even what he has will be taken away. As for this good-for-nothing servant, throw him out into the dark, where there will be weeping and grinding of teeth." '

Matthew 25:14-3

How careful have we been in our stewardship of the many gifts God has given to us? Where have we used our gifts for the building up of the Kingdom here on earth, for the good of the Church and for the good of each other?

Let all of us then live together in oneness of mind and heart,
mutually honouring God in ourselves,
whose temples we have become.
Amen.

From the Rule of St. Augustine (c. 40

Paul understood himself to be an apostle, an agent of some higher authority. Many of Paul's letters begin with a declaration of his apostolic status (Galatians 1:1; 1 Corinthians 1:1; 2 Corinthians 1:1; Romans 1:1; Colossians 1:1). This tradition was continued in the later letters (Ephesians 1:1; 1 Timothy 1:1 and 2 Timothy 1:1) whose authorship is uncertain. Paul is clear that he is an ambassador 'through Jesus Christ and God the Father' (Gal. 1:1). For him being an apostle conferred an 'office', within God's plan of salvation through Christ, and a particular commission to evangelise among the Gentiles (Gal. 1:16). Paul's apostolic ministry brought him great suffering. He calls himself a slave of Christ (Rom. 1:1 and Gal. 1:10), one with no rights except those granted to him by Christ. He identifies his suffering apostleship to the sufferings of Jesus (1 Cor. 4:8-13; Gal. 6:14 and 6:17).

Paul's claim to apostolic status was not unproblematic. He had been a virulent persecutor of Christians and whereas his claim to apostolic status rested on a vision of the Risen Jesus (Gal. 1:12) the other apostles, had seen Jesus in the flesh, being called by him during Christ's earthly life. This difference between Paul and the other apostles seems not to have concerned him. On one hand, he stressed his independence (Gal. 1:17), on the other he recognised the 'pride of place' to be given to those who were apostles before him (Gal. 1:17; 1 Cor. 15:4-10).

Paul usually calls Peter by his Jewish name, Cephas. In Galatians he recalls a quarrel that they had over the table fellowship between Jewish and Gentile believers at Antioch (Gal. 2:11-14a). Paul had a universalistic understanding of his mission, 'all are one in Christ Jesus' (Gal. 3:28) as a result of baptism. Therefore he could not understand how Cephas could refuse to share food with Gentiles. In due course Peter seems to have changed his mind: witness the incidents in the house of Cornelius (Acts 10:1-43). Historically, the alleged division in early Christianity between Paul and Peter has been exaggerated. United in faith, both Paul and Peter were martyred in Rome under the persecution of the Emperor Nero.

Opening Prayer

Leader:	How lovely is your dwelling place,
O Lord of hosts!
My soul longs, indeed it faints
for the courts of the Lord;
my heart and my flesh sing for joy
to the living God.

Group:	Even the sparrow finds a home,
and the swallow a nest for herself,
where she may lay her young,
at your altars, O Lord of hosts,
my King and my God.

Leader:	Happy are those who live in your house,
ever singing your praise.

Group:	For a day in your courts is better
than a thousand elsewhere.
I would rather be a doorkeeper in the house of my God
than live in the tents of wickedness.

From Psalm 8

All:	Glory be to him whose power, working in us, can do
infinitely more than we can ask or imagine; glory to
him from generation to generation in the Church and
in Christ Jesus for ever and ever. Amen.

Ephesians 3:20-2

*Let us listen carefully to the Word of the Lord,
and attend to it with the ear of our hearts.
Let us welcome it, and faithfully put it into practice.*

St. Benedict of Nursia (c.480-c.547) adapt

Exploring the Scriptures Colossians 2:20-23, 3:1-4

If you had really died with Christ to the principles of this world, why do you still let rules dictate to you, as though you were still living in the world? 'It is forbidden to pick up this, it is forbidden to taste that, it is forbidden to touch something else'; all these prohibitions are only concerned with things that perish by their very use – an example of human doctrines and regulations! It may be argued that true wisdom is to be found in these, with their self-imposed devotions, their self-abasement, and their severe treatment of the body; but once the flesh starts to protest, they are no use at all.

Since you have been brought back to true life with Christ, you must look for the things that are in heaven, where Christ is, sitting at God's right hand. Let your thoughts be on heavenly things, not on the things that are on earth, because you have died, and now the life you have is hidden with Christ in God. But when Christ is revealed – and he is your life – you too will be revealed in all your glory with him.

Following a short period of silence you may wish to share an image, a thought, a phrase that has struck you.

Reflection

Very soon we will enter once more into the season of Advent. Initially the readings will focus on the end of the world and the Second Coming of Christ. Often, Christ's return at the end of time is spoken of in fearsome terms. Here, however, St. Paul implies that it is something to look forward to. 'You too', he says, 'will be revealed in all your glory with him'.

Paul's optimistic approach to the Second Coming is mirrored in his approach to death; 'my desire', he says, 'is to depart and be with Christ, for that is far better' (Philippians 1:23). Paul's optimism is rooted in an utter conviction about God's faithfulness; that 'the one who calls you is faithful' (1 Thessalonians 5:24), and in the belief that having strived to live in union with Christ on earth, Christ will keep company with us in death. 'The saying is sure: If we have died with him, we will also live with him; if we endure, we will also reign with him' (2 Timothy 2:11-12).

Pope Benedict takes up this theme in *Spe Salvi*, his recent encyclical on hope. Here the Holy Father speaks of Christ the Shepherd; he who is the way, the truth and the life, who, having journeyed through the valley of death, enables us to approach the same journey in hope.

> The true shepherd is one who knows even the path that passes through the valley of death; one who walks with me even on the path of final solitude, where no one can accompany me, guiding me through: he himself has walked this path, he has descended into the kingdom of death, he has conquered death, and he has returned to accompany us now and to give us the certainty that, together with him, we can find a way through. The realisation that there is One who even in death accompanies me, and with his 'rod and his staff comforts me', so that 'I fear no evil' (cf. Psalm 23:4) – this was the new 'hope' that arose over the life of believers. (*Spe Salvi*, 6)

If, as St Paul puts it, we are dead to the principles of this world, 'our eyes set on heaven', then death, judgement, heaven and hell – the so-called 'Last Things' – are to be embraced. Be slaves of righteousness, he says, for this will end in eternal life (Romans 6:17-23). Paul came to see that being right with God was not about the observance of rules and regulations, but about living in Christ. What this means, Paul makes clear again and again. It is the self-sacrificing love which stops our words and actions from being empty gestures (1 Corinthians 13:1-13); it's the acknowledgement of our being members of a community, the body of Christ, the Church, rather than isolated individuals (1 Corinthians 12:26); it's the life of prayer, of thankfulness to God (1 Thessalonians 4:14-22). Indeed, all that is required an openness to the working of his Holy Spirit; to what God wants to and will achieve in us if we but allow (*Ephesians 3:16-19*).

What, if any difficulties, do you have with Paul's optimistic approach to death? What has living in Christ meant to you? How has your experience of small communities reshaped your understanding of what it is to live in Christ?

Leader: Aloud or in the silence of our hearts let us bring to the Father our thanks (pause)…

Leader: In sorrow let us ask the Father for forgiveness (pause)…

Leader: With confidence let us entrust to the Father our cares and concerns (pause)…

Closing Prayer

Heavenly Father,
open our minds and hearts to the working of your Holy Spirit.
Enlightened by Truth and emboldened through Grace,
may faith overcome doubt, love conquer hatred,
hope shine through suffering,
and zeal mark our proclamation of the Good News
that St. Paul preached to the peoples of all nations.
We ask this through your Son Jesus Christ
who lives and reigns with you, in the unity of the Holy Spirit,
one God for ever and ever.
Amen.

You may wish to take a few moments to look at (1 Thessalonians 4:13-18, 5:1-22) in which St. Paul tells us to prepare for the coming of the Lord by 'holding fast to what is good'. You may also care to reflect on these passages too: (2 Thessalonians 2:1-2; 1 Timothy 4:1-10).

Read the Scripture from the 33rd Sunday in Ordinary Time (Year A) – 1 Thessalonians 5:1-6

You will not be expecting us to write anything to you, brothers, about 'times and seasons', since you know very well that the Day of the Lord is going to come like a thief in the night. It is when people are saying, 'How quiet and peaceful it is' that the worst suddenly happens, as suddenly as labour pains come on a pregnant woman; and there will be no way for anybody to evade it.

But it is not as if you live in the dark, my brothers, for that Day to overtake you like a thief. No, you are all sons of light and sons of the day: we do not belong to the night or to darkness, so we should not go on sleeping, as everyone else does, but stay wide awake and sober.

Background

One of the major issues in the Thessalonian church centred on the timing of Christ's return (*parousia*) as judge of the universe. It was believed that this would happen very soon. However, as Christian converts began to die people began to ask how those who had already died would meet Christ (1 Thessalonians 4:13). In the letter to the Thessalonians Paul, along with Silvanus and Timothy, reassures the church at Thessalonica. 'For this we declare to you by the word of the Lord, that we who are alive, who are left until the coming of the Lord, will by no means precede those who have died' (1 Thess 4:15). Paul and his co-authors also reminded their audience that the timing of Christ's return is known only to God (1 Thess. 4:15-17) and that they must be prepared and watchful for Christ's coming (1 Thess. 5:4).

Metaphors found in the Jewish tradition, such as 'the Day of the Lord' (Joel 2:1), 'the thief in the night' (Matthew 24:43), and the labour pains of pregnancy before childbirth (Jeremiah 4:31) serve to highlight the suddenness of Christ's return and the need for believers to live and behave as children of the light rather than darkness (I Thess. 5:4-5). Practically speaking, believers are to avoid drunkenness (I Thess. 5:6) and to get on with doing what needs to be done (I Thess. 4:11). Metaphorically, believers are to be armed like soldiers (I Thess. 5:8) in order that the battle for the faith might be won. Now, as then, we are challenged to live in two worlds; expectant for Christ's return, living as the Thessalonians were instructed to live but conscious, in the exercise of our mission and ministry, of Christ's ever-abiding presence (Matthew 28:20).

Almighty Father
you command us to awake from our slumbers,
to arise from the dead.
You made us not to be held prisoner in the underworld,
nor to be held captive in sin.
We are the work of your hands; we are fashioned in your image.
Help us to rise, and go forward;
for you in me and I in you,
together we are one undivided person.
Amen.

Adapted from a reading from an ancient homily for Holy Saturday

If you have really died with Christ (Colossians 2:20)

St. Paul was a faithful Jew, a Pharisee, for whom the way to God was through the strict observance of the Mosaic Law. With his conversion however, he came to see that the way to God was through Christ. Put simply, Paul did not convert to another God, rather he came to understand that Jesus was the promised Messiah – the Way, the Truth and the Life – who opened up the way to the Father. For Paul, Christ was no longer considered cursed because he had 'hanged on a tree' (Deuteronomy 21:23) but is seen as 'wisdom, virtue, holiness and freedom' (1 Corinthians 1:30).

It is because Paul came to understand Christ as the way to the Father that he objected to Jewish observances, such as circumcision, being imposed upon those Gentiles who came to believe. The proof of living in Christ was in the imitation of Christ's life rather than faithful adherence to the Law.

From Christifideles Laici

16. Life according to the Spirit, whose fruit is holiness (cf. Romans 6:22; Galatians 5:22), stirs up every baptized person and requires each to follow and imitate Jesus Christ, in embracing the Beatitudes, in listening and meditating on the Word of God, in conscious and active participation in the liturgical and sacramental life of the Church, in personal prayer, in family or in community, in the hunger and thirst for justice, in the practice of the commandment of love in all circumstances of life and service to the brethren, especially the least, the poor and the suffering.

Christ, innocent though you were,
you died once for our sins,
you died for the guilty, to lead us to God.
In the body you were put to death,
in the spirit you were raised to life.
For this we give thanks.

Adapted from the Responsory, Easter Octave: Friday, Divine Office

why do you still let rules dictate to you (Colossians 2:20)

In his letter to the Romans (7:19), St Paul concludes, 'For I do not do the good I want, but the evil I do not want is what I do'. How often, as we have tried to follow Christ, have we experienced a similar feeling; conscious of the personal failings that seem so well ingrained? Yes, we know how we would want to be, how we would like to act, but something less noble - fear, greed, pride, anger, jealousy - seems to dictate the pattern of our lives.

Let me love you,
my Lord and my God,
and see myself as I really am:
a pilgrim in this world,
a Christian called to respect and love
all whose lives I touch,
those in authority over me,
or those under my authority,
my friends and my enemies.
Amen.

Taken from 'The Universal Prayer', attributed to Pope Clement XI (1649-1721)

Today is the Feast of the Dedication of the Basilicas of Saints Peter and Paul. Just as it was in the time of Constantine (c.274-337), the two great pilgrimages sites of Rome remain the tombs, or memorials, of St. Peter upon the Vatican Hill and the tomb of St. Paul off the Ostian Way. Today the Church honours Peter the fisherman, the rock on which the Church is built and Paul the tentmaker, reformed persecutor of Christians and Apostle to the Gentiles. As we pray today we unite our thoughts with those praying at the tombs of these Apostles.

I had been going through a period of difficulty, compounded by a medical illness. I entered a crisis period marked by anguish, soul searching, self-loathing and desperate prayer and pleading with God too. I could see no way out until I woke up on the morning of 31st May 1979 to a new reality. I was totally at peace, filled with a deep assurance of being loved, a sense of the closeness of God to me. It was like a revelation. So there and then I committed my life to God, in sheer gratitude and joy for what had happened. I sustained a prayer life and developed a real hunger for reading Scripture. This new sense of God's closeness and his love for me persisted and grew. All this began to affect my attitude to myself, to others and my behaviour.

Although there have been other key moments I have come to realise that faith is a journey, a relationship and a mystery. I realise it is always a gift – from God who first loves us – but one that needs constantly to be responded to. For the most part with me it has been about fostering a steady and faithful life of discipleship with a commitment to personal prayer, sacramental participation, fellowship with other Christians, a growth in holy living, study of Scripture and other Christian writing, a commitment to Christian witness, service and mission and in all of this to seek to specifically know and do the will of God. In fact the times of greatest personal difficulty and disappointment have proved to be the most fruitful for my growth in Christ. I have made lots of mistakes and increasingly realise my frailty yet also the faithfulness and mercy of God.

Like Peter, I often find myself perplexed but confessing 'Lord, to whom else shall I go? You have the words of eternal life! (John 6:68)'. It is a joy but also a constant challenge just to be called to daily grow in my relationship with Christ, 'pressing on' as St. Paul puts it. It is a privilege to be caught up in the Mystery of Christ and somehow and very imperfectly, to be part of his body on earth, an instrument used by him to bring his love, truth and life to others.

My life has steadily been shaped in subtle but powerful ways by the Eucharist. The church takes us into the heart of the communion of saints, those living on earth and those with the Lord beyond the grave. I know my Christian journey would be impossible without this communion and their help, love and support. The church's sheer diversity has also been enriching, and I have benefited immensely from all sorts of contacts and involvement with different groups, religious orders, new communities and movements. The Holy Spirit is so rich and lavish in his distribution of gifts and the ways he works!

Andrew Brookes

Come Holy Spirit, fill the hearts of your faithful
and kindle in them the fire of your love.
Send forth your Spirit, and they shall be created.
and you shall renew the face of the earth.
Amen.

Let your thoughts be on heavenly things (Colossians 3:2)

Thinking of Heaven can be reassuring. Home of the Saints, who remind us that Christian living is possible, and of the angels, so often the bearers of good news that speaks of God's abiding care, Heaven, to paraphrase St Paul, is that everlasting home where questioning and uncertainty will cease and we will see God face to face (1 Corinthians 13:8-12; Philippians 3:20; 2 Corinthians 5:1). Yet, thinking about Heaven can also be frustrating What will it be like? Who else will be there? What will we do? How will I cope with living eternally? In the answering the inadequacy of our language and knowledge becomes all too clear.

Where knowledge fails St. Paul invites us to trust in the Holy Spirit for it is only through the Spirit that we can begin to comprehend what God, in his goodness, has given us. 'What no eye has seen, nor ear heard, nor the heart of man conceived, what God has prepared for those who love him these things God has revealed to us through the Spirit; for the Spirit searches everything, even the depth of God' (1 Corinthians 2:9-10).

From the Catechism

1024. This perfect life with the Most Holy Trinity - this communion of li and love with the Trinity, with the Virgin Mary, the angels and all the blessed - is called 'heaven.' Heaven is the ultimate end and fulfilment of the deepest human longings, the state of supreme, definitive happiness.

O God in whom is all consolation,
who doth discern in us nothing that is not thine own gift,
grant me, when the term of this life is reached, –
the knowledge of the first truth,
the enjoyment of your Divine Majesty.
Amen.

St. Thomas Aquinas (c.1225-127

he is your life (Colossians 3:4)

In his letter to the Philippians St. Paul reminds us that life in Christ is the only life worth living. 'I have suffered the loss of all things, and I regard them as rubbish,' he says, 'in order that I may gain Christ and be found in him' (Philippians 3:8-9). Paul clings to Christ because Christ had already made Paul his own. As one translation of the Bible puts it, 'I press on till I conquer Christ Jesus, as I have already been conquered by him' (Philippians 3:12). Just as he claimed Paul, Christ has claimed us in the waters of baptism. For us being claimed by Christ for himself, being 'owned' by Christ, is all privilege for it opens up for us the way to eternal life. 'He is your life' says St. Paul, and the question in the face of today's text is a simple one…is he? And, if Christ is your life, how will others know?

Jesus, Way between the Father and us, I offer you all and await all from you.
Jesus, Way of sanctity, make me your faithful imitator.
Jesus Way, render me perfect as the Father who is in heaven.

Jesus Life, live in me, so that I may live in you.
Jesus Life, do not permit me to separate myself from you.
Jesus Life, grant that I may live eternally in the joy of your love.

Jesus Truth, may I be light for the world.
Jesus Way, may I be example and model for souls.
Jesus Life, may my presence bring grace and consolation everywhere.

From 'Invocations to the Divine Master' by Blessed James Alberione,
Practices of Piety and the Interior Life

Jesus said to his disciples: 'When the Son of Man comes in his glory, escorted by all the angels, then he will take his seat on his throne of glory. All the nations will be assembled before him and he will separate men one from another as the shepherd separates sheep from goats. He will place the sheep on his right hand and the goats on his left. Then the King will say to those on his right hand, "Come, you whom my Father has blessed, take for your heritage the kingdom prepared for you since the foundation of the world. For I was hungry and you gave me food; I was thirsty and you gave me drink; I was a stranger and you made me welcome; naked and you clothed me, sick and you visited me, in prison and you came to see me." Then the virtuous will say to him in reply, "Lord, when did we see you hungry and feed you; or thirsty and give you drink? When did we see you a stranger and make you welcome; naked and clothe you; sick or in prison and go to see you?" And the King will answer, "I tell you solemnly, in so far as you did this to one of the least of these brothers of mine, you did it to me." Next he will say to those on his left hand, "Go away from me, with your curse upon you, to the eternal fire prepared for the devil and his angels. For I was hungry and you never gave me food; I was thirsty and you never gave me anything to drink; I was a stranger and you never made me welcome, naked and you never clothed me, sick and in prison and you never visited me." Then it will be their turn to ask, "Lord, when did we see you hungry or thirsty, stranger or naked, sick or in prison, and did not come to your help?" Then he will answer, "I tell you solemnly, in so far as you neglected to do this to one of the least of these, you neglected to do it to me." And they will go away to eternal punishment, and the virtuous to eternal life.'

Matthew 25:31-

Living the 'virtuous' life which Jesus maps out for us is a real challenge. Reflecting on this gospel passage we may well ask ourselves, where and how have we neglected to serve Christ? Yet, the gospel is not given to us to burden us, it is given to us to lighten our way. This Advent we will hear again John the Baptist's invitation to repent. It is for this reason that our reading of the gospel can be coloured by hope.

God of your goodness, give me yourself,
for you are sufficient for me.
If I were to ask for anything less
I should always be in want,
for in you alone do I have all.
Amen.

Julian of Norwich (1342–1416)

Stages in Paul's thought

We can divide Paul's letters into three groups and by doing this it is possible to glimpse stages in the development of his thought.

Stage One – Paul's letters while on active missionary service (c. AD 50-5

a) I Thessalonians and (probably) 2 Thessalonians in which Paul discuss issues relating to Christ's return to the world as judge.

b) Galatians – Paul's most personal and heated letter which maintains that we can be made righteous before God in Christ without recourse to the Jewish Law especially in relation to circumcision.

c) The Corinthian correspondence represents Paul's most lengthy writings (29 chapters are preserved). Here Paul discusses his apostleship and living the Christian life in an urban environment.

d) Romans, continues some of the ideas found in Galatians and was written to advance Paul's evangelistic campaign to Spain by enlisting the support of the Roman church.

Stage Two – Paul's letters from prison (c. AD 58-65?)

a) Philippians, written to one of his favourite churches in which Paul argue that the humility of the Philippian church should model that of Christ.

b) Philemon, written to a friend asking that he receives back into his household the runaway slave, Onesimus.

c) Colossians, in which Paul addresses questions relating to following Chri and living the Christian life.

d) Ephesians, has some common features with Colossians but it is sometimes thought that Ephesians was written after Paul's death by a disciple. If we wish to detect how Paul's thought has developed it may b that we should consider his understanding of the Church by comparing Ephesians with I Thessalonians.

Stage Three – Paul's letters about succession (AD 65-80?)

1 Timothy, 2 Timothy and Titus – These letters may have been written (even in part) by Paul before his martyrdom or by a disciple who wished to maintain Paul's spiritual legacy. Again we must compare how Paul's thought has developed with regard to ministry by comparing these 'Pastoral letters' to 1 Thessalonians and Galatians.

Opening Prayer

Leader:	Give ear, O my people, to my teaching; incline your ears to the words of my mouth.
Group:	I will open my mouth in a parable; I will utter dark sayings from of old, things that we have heard and known, that our ancestors have told us.
Leader:	He commanded our ancestors to teach to their children; so that they should set their hope in God, and not forget the works of God, but keep his commandments;
Group:	We will not hide them from their children; we will tell to the coming generation the glorious deeds of the Lord, and his might, and the wonders that he has done.

From Psalm

All:	Glory be to him whose power, working in us, can do infinitely more than we can ask or imagine; glory to him from generation to generation in the Church and in Christ Jesus for ever and ever. Amen.

Ephesians 3:20-

Let us listen carefully to the Word of the Lord,
and attend to it with the ear of our hearts.
Let us welcome it, and faithfully put it into practice.

St. Benedict of Nursia (c.480-c.547) adap

Explore the Scriptures Romans 10:8-17

The word, that is the faith we proclaim, is very near to you, it is on your lips and in your heart. If your lips confess that Jesus is Lord and if you believe in your heart that God raised him from the dead, then you will be saved. By believing from the heart you are made righteous; by confessing with your lips you are saved. When scripture says: those who believe in him will have no cause for shame, it makes no distinction between Jew and Greek: all belong to the same Lord who is rich enough, however many ask for his help, for everyone who calls on the name of the Lord will be saved.

But they will not ask his help unless they believe in him, and they will not believe in him unless they have heard of him, and they will not hear of him unless they get a preacher, and they will never have a preacher unless one is sent, but as scripture says: The footsteps of those who bring good news is a welcome sound. Not everyone of course listens to the Good News. As Isaiah says: Lord, how many believed what we proclaimed? So faith comes from what is preached, and what is preached comes from the word of Christ.

Following a short period of silence you may wish to share an image, a thought, a phrase that has struck you.

Reflection

You are a son or daughter of God. The way we live our lives is to be determined by this simple but mind-blowing truth. All too easily such words can seem like a basic platitude, a phrase that slips off the tongue in sermons or reflections such as this but Stop! Consider! Be moved! The Creator of all invites us to enter into a deeply personal relationship.

Of this we can be justifiably proud; it is 'no cause for shame'. All too frequently we can be embarrassed when talking of our faith, consciously avoiding situations where we may have to reveal what we do on a

Sunday morning when the rest of the world is sleeping or washing the car. As children of God, gifted with the Holy Spirit in baptism and strengthened through confirmation, the Spirit of truth which the world does not understand nor perceive (John 14:17) remains our Advocate. Accompanied as we are by God's Spirit we have strength enough to accomplish the mission entrusted to us, 'to proclaim the Good News to all creation' (Mark 16:16), whether from the mountain tops as Moses di (Exodus 33:19), the housetops (Luke 12:3) or at the bus stop.

How do we go about doing this? How can we spread the message to those who need Christ's help, who do not yet believe, who have not yet heard? St. Paul writes that 'for the weak he made himself weak,' he 'mad himself all things to all men in order to save some at any cost'(1 Corinthians 9:22). Motivated by love, we must try to understand the complexity of people's situations. Again, in attempting to witness to Christ, we must be conscious that many do not speak 'our' language an that of the Church. The Second Vatican Council's Pastoral Constitution on the Church in the Modern World, Gaudium et Spes (GS), said that the Church and by extension those in the Church should talk 'in language intelligible to each generation' in order to 'respond to the perennial questions which are asked about this present life and the life to come' (GS, 4). We are called to live in the world so as to understand it and respond in love. Of course, living in the world is not to be 'of the world'. We live in the world, and seek to understand it, so as to challenge its values all the more effectively, and to reshape it according to Christ.

St. Paul wrote and spoke to real people, in real situations. Paul was concerned about empty gestures, idolatry and sexual ethics (1 Corinthians 5-11). What would he write about today?

Of all the things that concern you in this world today, what would be the one thing that you would like to change? How in this particular situation could you as an individual, as a group, show God's love in a language understood by the world at large?

Leader: Aloud or in the silence of our hearts let us bring to the Father our thanks (pause)…

Leader: In sorrow let us ask the Father for forgiveness (pause)…

Leader: With confidence let us entrust to the Father our cares and concerns (pause)…

Closing Prayer

Heavenly Father,
open our minds and hearts to the working of your Holy Spirit.
Enlightened by Truth and emboldened through Grace,
may faith overcome doubt, love conquer hatred,
hope shine through suffering,
and zeal mark our proclamation of the Good News
that St. Paul preached to the peoples of all nations.
We ask this through your Son Jesus Christ
who lives and reigns with you, in the unity of the Holy Spirit,
one God for ever and ever.
Amen.

Take a few moments to ponder (2 Corinthians 5:20-6:2), where Paul describes our role and our duty as baptised Christians in a world that is in desperate need of the one who sends us, Christ Jesus.

You may also care to reflect on (Philippians 4:6) and (2 Thessalonians 2:13-3:5).

Read the Scripture from Christ the King (Year A) –
1 Corinthians 15:20-26.28

Christ has been raised from the dead, the first-fruits of all who have fallen asleep. Death came through one man and in the same way the resurrection of the dead has come through one man. Just as all men die in Adam, so all men will be brought to life in Christ; but all of them in their proper order: Christ as the first-fruits and then, after the coming of Christ, those who belong to him. After that will come the end, when he hands over the kingdom to God the Father, having done away with every sovereignty, authority and power. For he must be king until he has put all his enemies under his feet and the last of the enemies to be destroyed is death. And when everything is subjected to him, then the Son himself will be subject in his turn to the One who subjected all things to him, so that God may be all in all.

Background

In 1 Corinthians 15 Paul addresses the notion of resurrection, a belief which some of the Corinthian Christians doubted (1 Cor. 15:12). Belief in the resurrection of Christ is the starting point for reflection upon the resurrection of Christian believers. For this purpose Paul uses the harvest metaphor of 'the first fruits' (1 Cor. 15:20, 23). Christ's resurrection prepares the way for the abundant 'crop' of the resurrection of the faithful. As our resurrection is dependant on that of Christ, so his resurrection was dependent on God's mighty action. In this passage God's power and might is the recurring theme (1 Cor. 15:24, 27, 28).

As resurrection marks the victory over sin and death Paul discusses human alienation from God by contrasting the actions of Adam (Hebrew for man) with those of Christ (cf. Romans 5:15-20). Through disobedience to God's will (Gen. 3:11) Adam brought death to all humanity (Genesis 3:22; 1 Cor. 15:22a). As a result of his obedience Christ brings resurrection from death and the offer of eternal life

(1 Cor. 15:22b). Although Christ has won salvation for us through his saving death and resurrection, and although through the sacraments and in the Church we enter into this, the totality of the experience of being saved awaits us in heavenly glory (cf. *Lumen Gentium*, 48).

Gracious God,
look upon a sinner who is yet created in your image.
Look upon a disciple into whose heart you gaze.
Look upon a child who longs to love you
with a heart yet more perfect,
and looking, forgive,
and gazing, pardon and bless;
for your truth and your mercy's sake.
Amen.

François Fenelon (1651-1715)

The word, that is the faith we proclaim, is very near to you, it is on your lips and in your heart. (Romans 10:8)

Is it really possible to 'lose' one's faith? Certainly, it is easy to think of our faith, whether we have it or whether we have 'lost' it, as depending on ourselves – what we do or don't do. Yet faith is not something we achieve, reach or obtain. Faith is God's gift. Like any gift it something that we can unwrap, explore and use; or something we can leave aside, unexplored and forgotten.

Ultimately, God will not take back his gift of faith (cf. Romans 11:29). As today's text reminds us 'the faith we proclaim, is very near, it is on your lips and in your heart'. Simply put, God is ever-present, searching and probing the depths of our heart. The question is not whether we have lost faith, but where and how we fail to respond to his Word alive and active in us (Hebrews 4:12-13).

God and Father,
to those who go astray you reveal the light of your truth
and enable them to return to the right path:
grant that all who have received the grace of baptism
may strive to be worthy of their Christian calling,
and reject everything opposed to it.
Through Christ our Lord.
Amen.

Concluding Prayer, Eastertide Mondays Weeks 2 to 6, Divine Office

all belong to the same Lord (Romans 10:12)

In his letter to the Romans, Paul reminds us that in Christ there are no distinctions between Jew and Greek, slave and citizen (Romans 10:12; cf. 1 Corinthians 12:12), 'the same Lord is Lord of all and is generous to all who call on him'. The Lord comes for everyone, sinners and saints alike, he does not discriminate as we might do.

We can be confident too that he cares for those he calls. As one of the Prefaces to the Apostles says: 'You are the eternal Shepherd who never leaves his flock untended', as sheep of his flock, 'we have no need to be afraid' (Luke 12:32). It is with this confidence in God's pastoral care that we can spread the gospel of Christ.

From Lumen Gentium (Christ, Light of Nations)

6. The Church is a sheepfold whose one and indispensable door is Christ (John 10:1-10). It is a flock of which God Himself foretold He would be the shepherd, (Isaiah 40:11 and Exodus 34:11) and whose sheep, although ruled by human shepherds; are nevertheless continuously led and nourished by Christ Himself, the Good Shepherd and the Prince of the shepherds,(John 10:11 and 1 Peter 5:4) who gave His life for the sheep (John 10:11-15).

Father, through Jesus our Lord and our brother, we ask you to bless us.
Grant that our parishes be true homes,
where everyone may find life,
where those of us who suffer may find hope.
Keep in your loving care all those who come.
Spirit of God, give us greatness of heart that we may welcome all those you send.
Make us compassionate that we may heal and bring peace.
Help us to see, to serve and to love.
Amen.

L'Arche prayer (adapted)

My relationship with God used to be very personal and private, and the very idea of talking about it to someone else would have filled me with horror! Fortunately, that has changed, but it took many years for that to happen. I was brought up a Catholic and had an outstanding Catholic education with 10 years at Stonyhurst, the Jesuit boarding school. At the age of 18 I was a speaker for the Catholic Evidence Guild where my talks were of dogma and doctrine. We were positively discouraged from including any personal testimony!

My faith was contained in a closed box and like many of my generation the thought of talking about one's relationship with God was unthinkable. While working and living in Nigeria, Malaysia, Hong Kong and China my family and I spent time with the exuberant and lively Christians of Africa and Asia and I was challenged by 'the dreaded sharing' at the lively home groups. God seemed to be so much more active in their lives!

It was during the three days of a Cursillo (Spanish for short course) in Christianity in Hong Kong that my isolation was challenged and that I came to see the real value, in fact the need to share with others. I realised that an isolated Christian is a paralysed Christian. During Cursillos we have three key subjects to review – our prayer life, what we are doing to improve our own spiritual formation, and what we are doing to evangelise others. I have learnt that it is the third subject, evangelisation, that really should be put first; the groups that thrive are the ones that consider evangelisation the key task. I have also learnt the power of prayer to give each other personal support. At these meetings I have learnt that prayer is answered. How else would I know?

Stephen F

On Thee do I set my hope, O my God,
that Thou shalt enlighten my mind and understanding
with the light of Thy knowledge,
not only to cherish those things which are written,
but to do them.
Thou art the enlightenment of those who lie in darkness,
and from Thee cometh every good deed and every gift.
Amen.

St. John Chrysostom (c. 347-407)

unless they have heard of him (Romans 10:14)

St. John Chrysostom wrote, in his tenth homily on St. Paul's first letter to Timothy, the following passage. It is a reminder of our vocation (1 Peter 2:9) and the power that living a Christian life can effect.

> 'He (Christ) left us on earth in order that we should become like beacons of light and teachers unto others; that we might act like leaven, move among men like angels, be like men unto children, and like spiritual men unto animal men, in order to win them over, and that we may be like seed, and bear abundant fruits. There would be no need for sermons, if our lives were shining; there would be no need for words, if we bore witness with our deeds. There would be no more pagans, if we were true Christians.'

In a world crying out for God, though it may not realise it, there is a very real need for believers to lead 'shining lives' so that people might be led to Christ, much as the magi were led to his manger by his star. Perhaps in the time leading up to Christmas, we might consider wearing an external symbol of our faith, a crucifix, a lapel pin or a badge and be ready to tell those who ask about the one whom God sent.

From Princeps Pastorum (Prince of the Shepherds)

32. Profession of the Christian faith is not intelligible without strong, lively apostolic fervour; in fact, 'everyone is bound to proclaim his faith to others, either to give good example and encouragement to the rest of the faithful, or to check the attacks of unbelievers,' (St. Thomas Aquinas) especially in our time, when the universal Church and human society are beset by many difficulties.

All this day, O Lord,
let me touch as many lives as possible for thee;
and every life I touch, do thou by thy spirit quicken,
whether through the word I speak,
the prayer I breathe,
or the life I live.
Amen.

Mary Sumner (1828-1921)

a welcome sound (Romans 10:15)

Think of the last time you opened a letter, received an email or answered a phone call from a friend. Was the message you received full of sadness or glad tidings? It is wonderful to hear good news however it comes, from whatever source, indeed it is 'a welcome sound'. We too have a profound and joyous message to share. It is one of salvation, peace and love (Isaiah 52:7). This love, expressed in Christ's death for us, moved St. Paul so much that his life was dedicated to sharing it.

Let us all permit the Word of God and the love of Christ to move us in a similar way. May it transform us more fully as disciples of Jesus Christ, to have our lives converted by his death and resurrection, to realise that we are all called in a variety of ways just as St. Paul was appointed by God, chosen in our mother's womb to share what we have with others (1 Corinthians 1:1 and Galatians 1:15-16).

From the Catechism

1785. In the formation of conscience the Word of God is the light for our path, we must assimilate it in faith and prayer and put it into practice. We must also examine our conscience before the Lord's Cross. We are assisted by the gifts of the Holy Spirit, aided by the witness or advice of others and guided by the authoritative teaching of the Church.

Give us grace, almighty God,
so to unite ourselves in faith with your only Son,
who underwent death and lay buried in the tomb
that we may rise again in newness of life with him,
who lives and reigns for ever and ever.
Amen.

Concluding Prayer, Night Prayer Friday, Divine Office

Jesus said to his disciples: 'Be on your guard, stay awake, because you never know when the time will come. It is like a man travelling abroad: he has gone from home, and left his servants in charge, each with his own task; and he has told the doorkeeper to stay awake. So stay awake, because you do not know when the master of the house is coming, evening, midnight, cockcrow, dawn; if he comes unexpectedly, he must not find you asleep. And what I say to you I say to all: Stay awake!'

Mark 13:33-37

As we enter into Advent we will be reminded of the need to 'stay awake', alert for the coming of the Lord. In the light of the last six weeks of reflection, is there a particular resolution you might make to help you in this? You may want to read the letters of St. Paul – perhaps taking a letter at a time and a chapter each day.

God our Father,
You taught the gospel to all the world
through the preaching of Paul your apostle.
May we who celebrate his conversion to the faith
follow him in bearing witness to your truth.
We ask this through our Lord Jesus Christ, your Son,
who lives and reigns with you and the Holy Spirit,
one God, for ever and ever.
Amen.

Opening Prayer The Conversion of St. Paul, Apostle (25 January), Roman Missal (1974)

As for me, my life is already being poured away as a libation, and the time has come for me to be gone. I have fought the good fight to the end; I have run the race to the finish; I have kept the faith; all there is to come now is the crown of righteousness reserved for me, which the Lord, the righteous judge, will give me on that Day; and not only to me but to all those who have longed for his Appearing (2 Timothy 4:6-8).

Notes

Notes

Notes

Notes